Jeord Stuart
Gender: Male
Position: Third-Born Prince
Personality: Secretly terrible on the inside
Magic Element: Fire
Specialty: Is a genius capable of anything
Signature Moves: Fake Smile, Intimidation

Katarina Claes
Gender: Female
Position: Eldest daughter
Personality: Pure and de
Magic Element: Earth
Specialty: Tree-Climbing
Signature Moves: Charm

Start Game?

➡YES

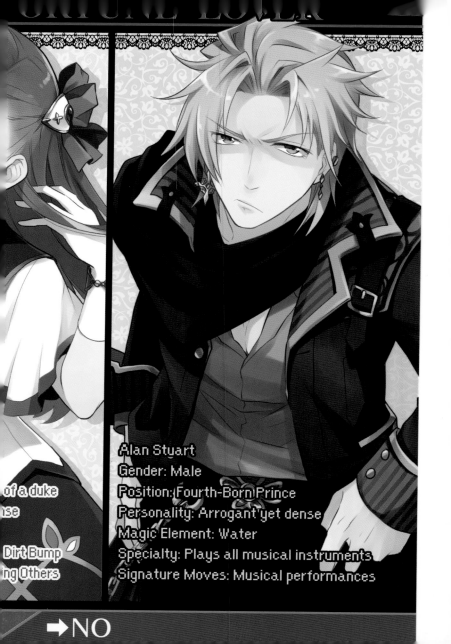

of a duke
se

Dirt Bump
ng Others

Alan Stuart
Gender: Male
Position: Fourth-Born Prince
Personality: Arrogant yet dense
Magic Element: Water
Specialty: Plays all musical instruments
Signature Moves: Musical performances

➔NO

My Next Life as a VILLAINESS: ALL ROUTES LEAD TO DOOM!

VOLUME 1

SATORU YAMAGUCHI

ILLUSTRATIONS BY NAMI HIDAKA

My Next Life as a Villainess: All Routes Lead to Doom! Volume 1
by Satoru Yamaguchi

Translated by Shirley Yeung
Edited by Aimee Zink

Copyright © 2015 Satoru Yamaguchi
Illustrations by Nami Hidaka

First published in Japan in 2015 by Ichijinsha Inc., Tokyo.
Publication rights for this English edition arranged through Kodansha Ltd., Tokyo.

Find more books like this one at www.j-novel.club!

President and Publisher: Samuel Pinansky
Managing Editor: Aimee Zink

ISBN: 978-1-7183-6660-2
Printed in Korea
First Printing: May 2020
10 9 8 7 6 5 4 3 2

Contents

My Next Life All Routes

Jeord Stuart

The third prince of the kingdom, and Katarina's fiancé. Although he looks like a fairy-tale prince with his blonde hair and blue eyes, he secretly harbors a twisted and terrible nature. He once spent his days in boredom, never showing interest in anything, until he met Katarina Claes. His magical element is Fire.

Katarina Claes

The only daughter of Duke Claes. Has slanted eyes and angled features, which she thinks make her look like a villainess. After her memories of her past life returned, she transformed from a spoiled noble lady to a problem child. Although she often gets ahead of herself, she is an honest and straightforward girl. She has below-average academic and magical ability. Her magical element is Earth.

Young Katarina

as a Villainess: Lead to Doom!

Character Introduction

Keith Claes

Katarina's adopted brother, taken in by the Claes family due to his magical aptitude. Considerably handsome, and seen by others as a "chivalrous ladies' man." His magical element is Earth.

Alan Stuart

Jeord's twin brother, and the fourth prince of the kingdom. Wildly handsome but also surly and arrogant. Often compares himself to his genius brother, and sulks when he realizes he can't catch up. His magical element is Water.

Mary Hunt

Fourth daughter of Marquis Hunt, and Alan's fiancée. Has lost her confidence and become withdrawn due to bullying by her older sisters.

Nicol Ascart

Son of Royal Chancellor Ascart. An incredibly beautiful and alluring young man who loves his sister, Sophia, deeply. His magical element is Wind.

Sophia Ascart

Daughter of Royal Chancellor Ascart, and Nicol's younger sister. Faces discrimination due to her white hair and red eyes. A calm and peaceful girl.

Luigi Claes

Duke, and head of the Claes Family. Katarina's father. Spoils his daughter.

Milidiana Claes

Katarina's mother, and wife of Duke Claes. Has very angled features, much like her daughter.

Anne Shelley

Katarina's maid, who's been with her since childhood.

One evening, I got carried away and ended up playing games late into the night. Of course, I overslept the next morning.

I changed into my uniform and washed my face half-heartedly, not even bothering to fix my frumpled hair before heading for the door. My mom complained that, as a high-schooler, I should at least try to be presentable. But I ignored her.

I rushed out the front door and jumped onto my trusty bicycle, which I'd used since middle school. With a strong kick to the pedals, I was off. I continued pumping with all my might, down the slope that merged into the main road.

Again and again I pedaled — *Maybe a little faster is better*. I kept going. As you might expect, I eventually reached a point where I could no longer control my speed.

My bicycle then decided it was a good idea to fly straight into the intersection of the busy main road.

As I slowly started blacking out from the inevitable impact, the distant and familiar voices of my family echoed through my mind: *"You idiot!"*

…At least, that was what I remembered of my previous life, having remembered it suddenly after a solid blow to the head.

Katarina Claes; eight years of age. As the only daughter of Duke Claes, I was spoiled and doted upon lovingly since I was born. Arrogant and selfish, I was the very image of a wealthy little lady.

Today, I was accompanying my father on a visit to a castle. The third prince of the kingdom, who was the same age as me, was to guide me through the castle gardens.

The very first time I met this prince, I was captivated by his blue eyes and golden hair. He had the face of an angel, too. His calm and composed demeanor was really something else — it was hard to believe he was only eight years old.

As you might expect, this self-indulging young lady immediately fell head over heels for the prince and stuck to him like glue. Said young lady was raised under the loving care of her parents, and was far too spoiled to care whether she was causing trouble for others.

I was following a little too closely after the prince, not looking where I was going, and I ended up bumping into him and falling over. I wasn't running when I tripped, but I couldn't have chosen a worse place to land. I fell head-first into a decorative rock in the garden and cracked my forehead open. There was enough blood gushing from the wound that it made the prince and the servants around us start to panic.

But personally, the bleeding was the last thing on my mind. The impact had made me regain the memories of a previous life, one where I was a seventeen-year-old high-school girl. In other words, seventeen years' worth of memories flooded my young mind in a flash — I felt like my brain would overload and shut down.

I was carried to the castle's infirmary while still completely dazed. After some preliminary treatment, I was transported back to Claes Manor. After that, my poor head was assaulted by a high-temperature fever for the next five days.

As the fever eventually subsided, I was able to organize the memories in my mind, and could finally sit up in bed. It was at that time that I received an unexpected visit from the prince himself. Due to the fact that I was still basically bedridden, the prince visited me in my chambers.

"Hello, Lady Katarina. I hope you are doing a little better." The angelic voice of the third prince, Jeord, only served to compliment his impossibly beautiful features. *What a charming face!*

While Katarina herself did have feelings for Prince Jeord prior to regaining her memories, I didn't exactly feel the same way, especially since I was mentally seventeen. But though I didn't have romantic feelings for the prince, looking upon his angel-like visage was enough to bring some peace to my mind.

I was so caught up in enjoying the sight of that pretty face that I forgot to answer him. The prince, who couldn't possibly imagine that this was the reason for my silence, gave me an even more preoccupied look.

"...Truly, I do apologize. To think that I was careless enough to have scarred your face..." the prince said, lowering his head.

This had all been my fault to begin with, since I was the one who was so self-absorbed that I'd followed behind him without watching where I was going. In fact, I even got my blood all over that gorgeous garden! I was the one who should have been apologizing.

Panicking, I responded quickly. "Please raise your head, Prince Jeord. I am fully responsible for my actions in this matter — in fact, I should apologize for inconveniencing you and the kind people at the castle..." I lowered my head apologetically, much to the surprise of Prince Jeord.

Come to think of it, the prince's only impression of me was that of a selfish eight-year-old. In the next five days, the prince's surprised expression was reflected on the faces of my family's servants too.

To be fair, Katarina was treated like a princess, and raised with an abundance of care. It would only be natural for her to put on airs and act in a manner befitting her station. But now with approximately seventeen years' worth of commoner memories in my head, I couldn't act all haughty like Katarina used to. Due to this, rumors of the young lady's personality abruptly changing due to the fever started spreading throughout the household.

Even Prince Jeord, who had only met me once, seemed surprised by this stark contrast in personality. Being the princely boy he was, however, he soon recovered from his initial shock.

"Not at all, my lady. If I had been more careful and observant of my surroundings, I would not have bumped into you, and perhaps you would not have ended up with a scar on your beautiful face. Please accept my humble apologies," he said, bowing his head deeply.

Ah, such a charming prince... Unlike the selfish Lady Katarina of the Claes household.

Indeed, my accident and the resulting injury did require a small stitch to treat, and a small scar — only a centimeter or so long — was left on my forehead. I didn't mind, though. I'm not trying to brag or anything, but I was a rowdy kid in my past life. When I was in elementary school, I'd run around the hills behind my house with my two big brothers. I injured myself multiple times, and sometimes I'd needed way more stitches than this. My mom protested at first, but she eventually gave up and stopped commenting altogether.

So anyway, it would have been silly to care about a small scar on my forehead. "No, not at all. Please don't worry about this, Your Highness. It is a small wound, one that can be easily hidden with my bangs! There is no problem at all," I said with a wide smile on my face. I didn't want to inconvenience the prince any more than I already had.

Prince Jeord's expression, however, once again froze into a mask of shock and disbelief. I looked around. The prince wasn't alone — all the servants in the room had similar looks plastered across their faces. An awkward atmosphere permeated the room.

The first to break the silence was the prince himself. *Ah, such maturity for an eight year old!* The 8+17 year old girl in the room would do well to learn from His Highness.

"…My lady, even if you do not see your injury as much of a concern, society would not view it so. In fact, this very injury may negatively impact any future engagements, or deter potential suitors."

"…Oh…" I replied, unsure of what else to say. In my previous world, there would never be such harsh penalties for such a tiny scar! Apparently, this wasn't the case in this medieval Europe-like world with its noble ladies and whatnot. In a world full of political marriages, even a small disadvantage could have a great impact. Noble society is really harsh.

As the reality of the situation dawned on me, I felt a deep melancholy wash over me as images of social debuts and other annoying responsibilities surfaced in my mind. For eight-year-old Katarina, debuting in society was a natural part of growing up. Now that I had my old memories, though, I couldn't see it as anything but a terrible drag.

After all, most of my time in grade school was spent climbing trees and trekking through the woods like a wild monkey. In middle school I became a full-fledged otaku, deeply immersing myself in manga, games, and anime. It wasn't exactly a fulfilling or purposeful lifestyle. How would someone like me debut in noble society?

Aah, I want to go back to my previous life… I wanna eat chips! And read manga! And watch anime! And play games!

"…rina. Lady Katarina…"

"…Oh. Yes?"

Lost in my memories of my past life, I had completely forgotten that Prince Jeord was standing before me. It would seem that he had quite a lot to say — unfortunately, I wasn't really listening. *Sorry, Prince Jeord…*

"Well then. Is that acceptable to you?"

"…Ah. Y-Yes. Of course."

The endearing prince was standing in front of me, looking straight into my eyes. Although I had hardly listened to anything he had to say, I nodded my head, beaming in response.

"Well then. I will visit you again once you are in better spirits. Do take care." He bowed, the very image of a sincere and charming eight-year old prince. He left my room with his entourage following behind him.

I wondered why the prince would want to visit me again. After all, I wasn't really listening. *I'll just ask the servants later.* With that thought in mind, I saw the prince off with a beaming smile.

With that, the prince's sudden visit was over. *Playing host to a visitor while feeling sick is really tiring. I guess I should sleep a little bit more. Goodnight…*

"Young miss! Congratulations!"

Although I had just lain back down, Anne, one of my maids, started shaking me to wake me up. *Just let me rest…*

Seemingly having held herself back earlier in Prince Jeord's presence, Anne was now shaking me with unbridled joy. Her face was bright red. *What is it, Anne? Have you lost your mind to Prince Jeord's charm?*

Anne, apparently not noticing my annoyed expression, continued gushing in elation. "Prince Jeord, despite being the third-born, is a most capable young man! And as the King freely chooses his successor from his children, there is a chance that he could inherit the throne! And you could very possibly become queen, being his fiancée! Congratulations on your engagement, young miss!"

Wait... what? What did she say? I felt like I'd heard her say something very strange. *Whose engagement?*

"Umm. Anne. What was that you said just now? Could you repeat it for me?"

"Yes, young miss! Since you are now engaged to Prince Jeord, you could very well become queen, too! Congratulations on your engagement!"

"...Who's engaged to who?"

"What are you talking about, young miss?! Of course I am referring to your engagement to Prince Jeord!"

"W... WHAAAAAT~?!" My scream reverberated through the manor's halls.

This scream, too, was eventually attributed to the toll that my fever had taken on my poor little head.

When I had finally calmed myself, I demanded to hear the details from Anne. To be specific, I asked her what exactly Prince Jeord had said while I was busy thinking about my past life.

Apparently the prince felt responsible for the scar on my forehead, so he had taken it upon himself to make amends. By amends, he meant his intention to take me as his bride. *No, no. Wait a minute. Prince Jeord is still eight!*

While I personally felt that this was way too early, it seemed to be the norm in this world, according to Katarina's original eight years' worth of memories. In fact, the engagement of Prince Jeord's brother, who was just two years older, had been announced less than half a year ago. Also, I was now Katarina Claes, the first daughter of Duke Claes. A noble marrying into royalty wouldn't be anything out of the ordinary.

I supposed there wasn't anything necessarily bad about this... I would be marrying an angelic prince, and maybe eventually even become queen. To the daughters of other nobles, this must be a dream-come-true scenario. Both my parents were overjoyed about this turn of events.

But I just felt like it was a huge hassle. I already hated the idea of social debuts — and now I was engaged to a prince and could eventually become queen? If that wasn't a hassle, what was?

Of course, it wasn't like I could turn the prince down now. Saying *"No, I don't want to do it!"* to my happy family and servants was impossible. I sighed deeply. *Even so... I can't believe that Prince Jeord would be this concerned over a small injury! Even when it was my own fault that I fell over in the first place... Did he have to go that far?*

I sighed again, raising a small hand-mirror to my face. Reflected in its surface was the exhausted face of a young girl with a tiny series of stitches on her forehead. If I had to say, Katarina was more beautiful than most people — at least, she was considerably more beautiful than how I looked in my previous life.

Katarina had a head full of silky smooth brown hair. Her aqua-blue eyes, slanted somewhat upwards, reminded me of something. All I had to do was curl up the edges of her thin lips... There! I looked just like a stereotypical villainess.

On the inside, I remained a terrible, ape-like otaku girl. It didn't take much thought to understand that I could never get along with anyone as smart and refined as Prince Jeord.

That day, I ended up letting out sigh after sigh.

Although I tried to talk to my parents about this a lot of times, they seemed to think my annoying behavior was a symptom of the fever and just told me to rest until I was better. With that, I confined myself to my room. On the bright side, I was resting in a bed that was three times bigger than mine in my past life.

On top of having a fever for the past week, the prince came to visit right after I woke up. I'd hardly had time to do anything, let alone review the memories of my past life. But now I was finally left alone with my own thoughts.

In my previous life, my father was an office worker and my mother juggled housekeeping with a part-time job. As the only girl in the family, I was showered with love and care. I spent most of my grade school days romping around the hills with my brothers. And then, when I met an otaku friend in middle school, I dove head-first into the otaku lifestyle. I spent most of my time buying and consuming manga, *doujinshi*, anime DVDs, and games. In fact, this continued all the way up to high school, where I started playing *otome* games that my friend recommended.

Come to think of it, I never managed to see all the endings of that one game I was playing... Specifically, it was an otome game that I had bought a few days prior to my unfortunate bicycle incident.

Hmm... Yeah. It was a game with a medieval European world and set in a magical academy. *Of course, how could I forget?* I liked this game so much that I'd spend all of my after-school time playing it, only stopping for meals and showers. The night before, I was saving and reloading again and again as I desperately tried to get the good ending with the terrible, black-hearted, sadistic prince character. I didn't have any luck, so I kept on reloading. Before I knew it, the sun had begun to rise.

Ugh, if only I had gone to sleep sooner... Why was I so fixated on reaching that ending? But the old adage was right; there was no use crying over spilled milk.

Sometime in the early hours of the morning, I had finally conquered the route of the prince with the fake smile. Although he looked like a total fairy-tale prince, on the inside he was a sadistic and wicked character. At least, that was how he was written.

Being perfect at everything he did, the prince was always bored by life. The protagonist then appears before him, blowing away his melancholy days with her bright and energetic personality. The prince takes a liking to her, and the situation evolves into a love story.

But since the prince was such a twisted character, it was super difficult to make him like you. To make things worse, the rival character in the prince's route was a huge pain. She was the daughter of a rich duke, and had been engaged to the prince since childhood.

This was because, when they were kids, the prince had bumped into her and caused her to trip and hurt her head. She then used the resulting scar as leverage to guilt him into marrying her. She keeps him bound to the engagement, bullying the protagonist and attempting to force the two apart.

In reality, the scar had disappeared a long time ago. While the wicked prince himself knew this, he planned to use the scar-less rival character as a means of defense against an endless stream of female suitors.

In any case, that rival character was really a piece of work — even *I* was annoyed while playing the game. *Hmm... Why does all this seem so familiar?*

Using a scar accidentally inflicted by a young prince to secure a beneficial marriage... The oldest daughter of a duke... Keeping the prince unwillingly bound to an engagement...

The sadistic prince character in this game was... his name was... Prince Jeord.

And the... the rival character's name was... Katarina Claes...?!

Panicking as the realization hit me, I sat up in my bed, raising the mirror to my face again. What I saw was, without any doubt, the face of the game's rival character — the villainess.

...This looks like the face of a villainess because it is *the face of a villainess... It can't be...*

"NO *WAY*—!"

For the second time that day, my screams reverberated throughout the manor. As a result, the main subject of the household gossip turned to whether the young lady would need another visit from the good doctor.

Anyway, I had to figure out if this was actually the world from the otome game I'd been playing. It could just be a coincidence — just because the names and setting matched didn't necessarily mean that I was in the same world! I shouldn't rush to conclusions.

The first thing I had to do was record on paper everything that I remembered about the game world. The game I had been playing up until my untimely death was called *Fortune Lover,* and was set in a medieval European-style kingdom, where people practiced both swordplay and magic. Mainly set in an academy dedicated to the study of the magic arts, it was a classic, romance-centric otome game.

Among the nobles in this world, some were born with the gift of magic. Sometimes commoners were blessed with it too, but that was incredibly rare. When a magic-wielder turned fifteen, they would enroll in this magic academy to learn how to better control their powers.

The protagonist was a commoner who was admitted into the academy despite her social status due to her rare talent in magic. Suddenly thrust into an academy filled with nobles, the bright and optimistic protagonist finds herself having to overcome all kinds of obstacles.

By the way, the magic types of this world were based on elements, and included the Fire, Water, Earth, Wind, and Light elements. Earth was the most common, followed by Wind, Water, and Fire. Light, the rarest one, was the strongest of the five elements, but wielders of it were extremely rare. The protagonist, of course, wielded Light Magic.

There were four possible romance options in the game, the first of which being the third prince of the kingdom, Jeord Stuart. I was taking on his route right before my unfortunate death. At first he seemed like a fairy-tale prince with his blonde hair and blue eyes. Unfortunately, he had a wicked and twisted personality, and was a genius who could easily do anything he put his mind to. He wasted away his days without much interest in anything. He also had a fiancée who was engaged to him ever since childhood — the oldest daughter of Duke Claes, Katarina Claes. His magical element was Fire.

The second love interest was Jeord's twin and the fourth prince of the kingdom, Alan Stuart. He had developed an inferiority complex because of his twin brother's outstanding capabilities, though he wasn't anywhere near as twisted as him. Unlike Jeord, he had silver hair and blue eyes, and had a somewhat wild, dashing atmosphere about him. As the youngest child in the royal family, he had a spoiled personality. His magical element was Water.

The third love interest was the adopted brother of Jeord's fiancée, Keith Claes. As his name suggested, Katarina Claes was his older adoptive sister. He had been adopted into the Claes family due to his outstanding magical potential. But his adoptive mother and older sister didn't welcome him into the family, and his childhood was mostly a lonely one. As a form of rebellion against this neglect, he eventually grew into a flirtatious playboy. His flaxen-beige hair and green eyes backed up his ladies' man image. His magical element was Earth.

The fourth and last love interest was Nicol Ascart, son of the Royal Chancellor and childhood friend of Jeord and Alan. Of the four, he was the closest to a normal person. But due to his ever-present poker face and his reserved nature, he was a difficult character to approach. He was considerably handsome with his black hair and dark eyes, and his magical element was Wind.

And then we come to the infamous rival character, Katarina Claes...

In the setting of this game, Katarina was the oldest daughter of Duke Claes, and had the prideful attitude to match. She sported a scar left on her forehead from an accident with Prince Jeord in her childhood, and was his fiancée under the justification that he belonged to her as long as the scar remained. The prince, in turn, was honor-bound by this arrangement. Katarina was a wicked and unkind person who bullied her adopted brother endlessly. Her magical element was Earth.

There was a reverse harem route in this game, where a player could actually get happy endings with all the potential love interests. But as for Katarina Claes...

While she was an obvious obstacle in the Jeord route, she also showed up to terrorize the protagonist in Keith's route, unhappy that her adopted brother was interested in a mere commoner. She did the same in the reverse harem route as well, and was an all-around rotten antagonist.

If the protagonist succeeded in the Jeord route and reached the proverbial happy ending, this dedicated villainess would be stripped of her status and expelled from the kingdom for her long history of petty crimes and bullying against the protagonist... After which the protagonist marries Jeord and lives happily ever after.

In the bad ending, however, she would attack the protagonist with a knife out of sheer jealousy. Jeord, jumping in to defend his love, ends up killing Katarina in response. Even if it was to protect someone he loved, Jeord ended up killing his fiancée, and leaves the kingdom in self-exile to embark on a long journey.

The same was true for the Keith's route and the reverse harem route, with Katarina the villainess either dying or being chased out of the kingdom.

Hmm...? That's a little weird, isn't it? In the happy endings, she gets chased out of the kingdom and stripped of her title... and in the bad endings, she dies... Are there no happy endings for Katarina Claes?! There are only bad endings! All routes lead to doom!

I moved my quill across the paper as quickly as I could, jotting down any and all information I could remember. Then, holding my papers in my hands, I gathered information from my parents and servants, before heading into the library to conduct detailed research on the history of this kingdom.

With my messy hair and bloodshot eyes, I ran from shelf to shelf. Concerned about my welfare, my parents and servants offered to call a doctor. But I had no time for that, so I flatly rejected their offers.

A few days later I finally arrived at my answer, but it left me at a complete loss. My investigations only confirmed my suspicions, and further digging yielded the one answer I did not want to arrive at. I had no choice but to believe the fruits of my labor.

This was indeed the world portrayed in *Fortune Lover*...

I had no choice but to believe that I had somehow been reborn into the world of the game I had been playing on the night before my death. This was the world of *Fortune Lover*. But if this was the case, there was no way I could sit around and accept the Bad Ends of Katarina Claes.

Honestly, being chased out of the kingdom or being killed in one way or another was not something I looked forward to. Given that my previous life had been so cruelly cut short, I should at least be able to live until a ripe old age in this life! Yes, with a cat on my lap and everything!

And so, we will now officially commence the first Bad End Avoidance Strategy Meeting.

Meeting chairwoman: Katarina Claes.

Meeting representative: Katarina Claes.

Meeting secretary: Katarina Claes.

...*I guess I have to somehow figure it out all by myself.* After all, I didn't have anyone to discuss this with. With the whole manor already concerned about my mental health, I couldn't exactly stand

21

up and announce to my parents and servants that *"I was actually reborn in the world of the otome game I was playing in my previous life!"* Between the wild look in my eyes and their confusion, I would definitely be dragged away by force to a hospital.

And so, without further ado, let the first Katarina Claes Catastrophic Bad End Avoidance Strategy Meeting commence.

"Well then. Do any of you ladies have any good ideas?"

"Yes."

"Alright. Well then, Miss Katarina Claes, if you would."

"Firstly, I think that it would be wise to break off the engagement with Prince Jeord. If we can achieve that, we would successfully avoid all of Jeord's Bad Ends of Doom."

"That is true, yes. But this offer was extended by Jeord himself... Could you bring yourself to shatter the happiness of your family?"

"... I suppose not."

"Well then... What if we simply don't attend classes at the magic academy? If we successfully avoid the protagonist, we would avoid all of the game's plot points!"

"Isn't going to the academy the duty of all those born with magical aptitude? In Katarina's case, her powers appeared at five years of age. Even if she is spoiled by her father, I don't think he would yield with regards to the academy..."

"Gah. All that trouble for this no-good, useless Earth Magic..."

"Well... How about we just not bully the protagonist in the first place?"

"Yes, yes that's right!"

"...In the game, didn't Katarina's flunkies end up bullying the protagonist too? Even if we don't bully her, we could be seen as the ringleader!"

"That's not all! Our fiancé is that twisted Prince Jeord! He may... *do something* about us, if only so that he can end up with the protagonist!"

"N-No... What do we do, then?"

"I don't want to die..."

"...What do we do if we get chased out of the country and lose our social standing...? I have no idea..."

"In any case, we should all calm down. I've just thought of an excellent idea."

"An excellent idea?!"

"First things first... If Jeord ever makes an attempt on our lives, we need to be able to defend ourselves. To that end, we have to become more skilled at the sword! If it comes down to it and we do have to fight him, we won't fall so easily to his blade!"

"Oooh! That's true!"

"Also... we will need some means of survival if we do get exiled from the kingdom. My suggested solution would be... improving our magical ability."

"And how exactly do we do that? Katarina only has that pathetic Earth Magic..."

"There aren't as many people with magical aptitude in other kingdoms. So... if we do practice and hone our magical skills, we would have no trouble finding employment even if we do get kicked out of the kingdom. In fact, Katarina was obsessed with Jeord in the game, and spent all her time trying to get into his good books... That's why her grades were bad! She didn't study or practice her magic at all! So, if we really put our minds to it, we can become skilled at magic!"

"Oh, I see!"

"That's exactly it!"

"Well then, ladies. The solution is clear — we are to put our minds to honing our swordplay and magic!"

"Agreed."

"Agreed."

And with this, the first Katarina Claes Catastrophic Bad End Avoidance Strategy Meeting came to an end.

If there were just one person in this meeting who wasn't Katarina Claes, they would be quick to point out that the solution the three Katarinas had arrived at wasn't really much of a solution at all. Unfortunately, there was no other person present to tell Katarina this very important point...

After the first Katarina Claes meeting, I started on my agenda the very next day, beginning with a special training regimen in swordplay and magic. While my parents were surprised by my sudden request, I claimed that it was because I wanted to learn self-defense, and that I didn't want to embarrass myself at the academy. My insistence eventually led to my parents agreeing, though they seemed somewhat exasperated. *Come to think of it, their expressions remind me of a face my previous parents used to make. How nostalgic...*

I pestered my blank-eyed father, convincing him to find me swordplay and magic tutors ASAP. While he did manage to find me an instructor for swordplay pretty quickly, a magic tutor was a little more difficult. And so I resigned myself to reading books on magic from the manor's library instead — for now, this would have to do.

In a corner of the garden, I propped up an old, thickly-bound tome on my knees, opening it and reading the very first page. Written on the page were the following words: *"To reach great heights in magic, one must first communicate with one's magical origins."*

I didn't exactly swing swords around or cast magic in my previous life. So there was no way I would suddenly become a magical prodigy in this world. In other words, I was starting from scratch.

Communicate with one's magical origins... My magical element was Earth. And to make things worse, my magic was pathetically weak. For reference, my one and only magical spell could raise up a spot of earth by two or three centimeters. In its current state, it was basically useless to me. In fact... Katarina Claes could not use any other kind of magic in the game — pushing up earth by miniscule levels was the best she could do.

This "make a bump of earth about two or three centimeters long" magic — I suppose we could call it "Dirt Bump" — was usually used to trip the protagonist. Was... Was there anything else? No? So, Dirt Bump was basically a tool that could trip people and not much else.

Terrible. A truly pathetic kind of magic. If this tiny Dirt Bump was all I could use, how would I escape the doomed fates before me?! I had to somehow improve my magical powers!

Communicate with one's magical origins... Hmm... Does that mean I have to speak with... the earth itself?

The earth... Communicate... Speak with the earth. OH! I see!

"Um... Young miss. What exactly is it that you are doing?" my maid Anne called out to me with a somewhat concerned expression.

"Oh, I'm tilling the earth!" I answered energetically, dressed in a set of overalls I had borrowed from one of the gardeners. On this day, I had decided to plant some crops in the manor's large garden.

"Umm. I do recall you wishing to practice your magic. But... why are you tilling the earth?"

"I'm tilling the earth and planting crops to increase my magical power, you see!"

"I sincerely apologize, but I do not profess to understand any of what you just said," Anne replied, her expression of concern now replaced by a surprised one. She seemed confused by my cheerful response.

"Umm, in this tome of magic I read, it said… 'To reach great heights in magic, one must first communicate with one's magical origins.' And my magical element is Earth, right? So this is it! I'm communicating with the earth! And I'm doing it while planting crops in the field!"

Actually, my previous mother's side of the family had a long history of farming. My grandmother used to say that tending to the fields was like speaking to the earth, and that was that. I was grateful for her advice now — if I succeeded in tilling this field and eventually reaped its harvest, I would achieve great communication with the earth.

Of course, I asked for permission from the gardener first, and then borrowed a hoe, shovel, and gardening overalls. I couldn't possibly be more prepared. As long as I kept honing my magical powers by tilling the fields, I would successfully avoid a Catastrophic Bad End.

"…I do not think that tilling the fields is 'communicating with one's magical origins'… Somehow, something feels… off, about that interpretation…"

Anne seemed to be mumbling to herself now. Leaving her to her own devices, I brought my hoe down to continue my effort to till the earth.

Only seven more years until I would start studying at the academy. During this time, I had to do more than just strengthen my Dirt Bump spell — I also had to learn other spells, preferably profitable ones. And so I continued working the small field I stood in, shoveling the dirt with a steely focus.

My field work was soon interrupted by Anne, however, who appeared to have suddenly recalled something important. "...Ahh! This isn't the time for you to be tilling the earth and working the fields, young miss! You have an important engagement — the prince... Prince Jeord is paying you a social visit today!"

"...Huh? Why?" I asked, dropping my hoe in surprise.

"What do you mean why, young miss?! He said he would visit you again to formally announce the engagement!"

"Oh... Did he?" *Oops.* It had totally slipped my mind...

"In any case, you mustn't keep him waiting! Please return to the manor at once!"

"Y-Yes! Let's do that!" I couldn't let the prince, of all people, see me in this getup. Even I knew that was a little too much.

Panicking, I turned and tried to head towards the mansion — but it was already too late. Impatient at my absence, Jeord and his entourage of servants had decided to visit me directly in the garden instead. The prince's servants seemed hesitant as they laid their eyes upon me, probably confused as to why a noble young lady, who was supposed to be practicing her magical skills, was dressed in a farming getup with a hoe at her feet.

What do I do...? Honestly, I had wanted to sneak back into the mansion undetected, change out of my overalls, and return to the garden with a fresh face. But of course, I couldn't do that now. Prince Jeord, the last person I wanted to see me in this getup, was staring right at me.

Judging by the prince's wide eyes, he seemed overcome with surprise at first. But he soon assumed his usual smile and called out to me. "If it isn't Lady Katarina. I heard that you were practicing your magic in the garden, and thought I would spectate. What exactly is it that you are doing?" the prince said, his ever-lovely smile plastered across his face.

While I would have called that smile angelic before, I now knew that Prince Jeord was the very same twisted and wicked prince from *Fortune Lover*. He was a true sadist, and his smile now seemed completely demonic. It was clear that he was laughing at me — a supposedly noble lady, standing in the middle of a field in gardening overalls. This was not the smile of a cute little prince who genuinely wanted to know what I was doing.

I turned to look at the servants of my household, and then to the prince's entourage. Yep. They were completely frozen, rooted to the ground. In fact, my father, who had come here with the prince's group, was now so pale that he seemed like he would pass out at any moment.

Actually, my mother had already passed out, and was currently being supported by her personal maidservants.

Since I was wearing this getup, there was no point in lying about what I was doing. I decided to ignore the frozen servants and my petrified parents and simply stated the truth.

"Good day, Prince Jeord. Thank you for coming all this way — I do apologize for the inconvenience. I am currently communicating with the origins of my magic: the earth."

"Ahem. Communicating with the earth?"

"Yes. I felt that the fastest and most efficient way to do so was to till the earth and work the fields, and so that was what I did."

"…So you are tilling the earth… to communicate with it? Working the fields… to talk to the earth?"

I had answered the prince truthfully and cheerfully, and topped it off with a slight smile. In response, the prince looked downwards, his shoulders trembling.

Oh no. Now I've gone and done it. Did it make him mad? Don't tell me I'll be exiled from the kingdom before I even get to the academy...! I swallowed hard.

After a while, the prince's shivering stopped and he raised his head, staring straight at me. There was a smile on his face. At least he didn't seem angry — that was a relief.

"I see. Tilling the earth and working the fields to improve one's magic... A truly revolutionary form of practice, to be sure."

"...Is that so...?" Being completely clueless about magic, I didn't even know whether it was revolutionary or not. So I gave him a vague response, hoping to smooth it over.

But then Prince Jeord suddenly approached me, stepping into the field I had been working on. With yet another unexpected motion, he knelt down before me, holding out his right hand.

"Lady Katarina — I am here on a formal visit to discuss the matter of our engagement. I hope you will overlook my rudeness for asking in such a place, but do you accept my proposal?"

"Oh... Um. Uh. Yes."

Jeord promptly took my hand in his, before lowering his head and planting a kiss on it. Just like a scene out of a fairy tale. The fact that one of the two was dressed in gardening overalls, however, didn't really fit the image.

Before I knew it, I had accepted the proposal of this angel-like prince. If I were any other noble's daughter, or perhaps even Katarina before her memories returned, I would have been elated. But for me, it was hard to believe that Prince Jeord had just planted a kiss on my dirt-stained hand. In fact, I should have rejected him, saying something along the lines of *"I am hardly worthy of you, Prince Jeord."*

Oh... Oh no! I was caught up in the moment and said yes by accident! Ugh! This is bad. I can't take it back now! What do I do?!

In fact, even my house-servants and Jeord's entourage seemed to be looking at us in a warm, congratulatory way! It was like Jeord's overwhelming charm had caused everyone to forget about the fact that I was in gardening overalls! Jeord's powers were truly fearsome.

Look! Even Father, who was almost out cold a few seconds ago, is clapping!

Ah. But Mother is still unconscious.

I have no idea how we got to this point, but I guess I'm now the official fiancée of Prince Jeord, the third-born son of the King. I guess all I can do is practice swordplay and magic even harder from now on...

My name is Jeord Stuart.

As the third-born son of the King, I am in a strange position. In this kingdom, the monarch chooses his successor. As such, I have a chance to become the next king of these lands, but honestly speaking, such a notion bores me. It seems like nothing more than a hassle.

To begin with, both of my older brothers are extremely capable, and are rivals to each other in studying and practicing with the sword. The next king in line should, naturally, be one of them. I also have a twin brother. Due to his naturally weak constitution since his birth, he was fussed over by the nursemaids and our mother, so I hardly spent any time with him growing up.

Such is my role in this unfortunate affair, with most of the attention spread between my two older brothers and my younger twin. Sometimes, it almost seems like the entire castle has forgotten about my very existence.

With minimal tutelage, I was able to master both the sword and my studies — while my tutors have much praise for me, what of it? It is meaningless to me.

I am skilled at reading the thoughts of others, and am well-loved by my tutors and superiors, gaining their favor with a simple, fabricated smile and a little flattery. Unlike my older brothers, I do not have much of a goal in life, and do not really experience hardship in most matters. Each day has been a requiem in boredom.

Amidst this boredom and repetition, however, I was dragged into quite the troublesome affair about half a year ago. To be precise, said event was the wedding engagement of my second oldest brother, perhaps spurred by my oldest brother's engagement a year ago.

None of that really mattered to me, however — no matter the number of announcements, they were all irrelevant to me… or so I thought.

Society's nobles, not having much else to gossip about, immediately focused on the possibility of the third prince getting engaged as well. While I was a largely forgotten presence at the castle, I remained popular in noble society, having paid my dues and performed the tasks expected of my role. Not a single noble in the relevant social circles had anything bad to say about Prince Jeord, third in line to the throne. As a result, a countless stream of potential brides were brought before me by their noble parents. This was, again, nothing but a hassle.

It was at this very moment that Duke Claes sent a missive to me, saying that he would be bringing his daughter to the castle on his next visit, and that he would very much like for me to meet with her; a common phenomenon. Noble parents commonly paraded their young daughters before me, expecting an offer of engagement if they should suit my tastes.

Due to the fact that Duke Claes wielded a significant amount of social and political strength, I could not exactly refuse — and eventually, the day arrived.

My first impression of the young Lady Katarina Claes was... as expected. She was a spoiled, prideful, arrogant, stupid young girl. She stuck to me like mud to the heel of a boot. Most annoying.

As a result of this selfish, self-induced behavior, she fell and hit her head. Truly troublesome. From what I heard, the impact had left a cut on her head, one that was deep enough to require stitching. *You reap what you sow* — that was what I thought when I heard the news. Well, I supposed a formal visit was in order, and then that would be the end of this affair.

"Lady Katarina Claes seems to have taken quite a liking to you, Prince Jeord. Do you not think that she could simply demand an engagement from you, using this injury as a front?"

A statement from one of the servants... *But yes, I can use that to my advantage.* Honestly, this endless line of female suitors and nobles parading their daughters before me was irritating. Although I just wanted to pick a bride at random, the norms of noble society would not forgive such a thing.

There were various political factions in noble society — both my older brothers had political factions of their own, as befitting of their station. If I were to take a noble lady from the political camp that sided with my oldest brother, my second oldest brother would ask if I had some intention to side with the other, and vice versa.

Conveniently enough, the Claes family was neutral, having pledged allegiance to neither of my brothers' camps. In addition, I now had a fitting excuse — that of having accidentally scarred their daughter. It would be difficult for anyone to think that the third prince, having allied himself with Duke Claes, was aiming for the throne.

The girl was, of course, sufficiently irritating, and would probably be easily fooled considering that she seemed to be a complete imbecile. With all these factors in mind, I decided to pay a visit to Lady Katarina, eldest daughter of the Claes family.

Upon entering the recovering Lady Katarina's room, what I heard betrayed my expectations...

"No, not at all. Please don't worry about this, Your Highness. It is a small wound, one that can be easily hidden with my bangs! There is no problem at all."

Katarina's unexpected, almost ridiculous response struck me with considerable force, leaving me momentarily speechless. *What is this girl on about?* It was as she said — the scar itself was neither large nor prominent. However... this was hardly something a noble lady would say.

To think that she was just a spoiled little noble girl when I had first met her... Was her fever this severe? Even so, suddenly going back on my elaborate plan would be even more troublesome. Katarina, with a cheerful but somewhat dazed expression on her face, did not really seem to be listening as I described the details of the proposal that she agreed to.

Katarina Claes… I now found myself somewhat interested in the girl. Perhaps it would be wise to observe her for a little longer.

And so it came to be that I paid Lady Katarina Claes a formal visit, as is custom for marriage engagements. Katarina, however, presented me with yet another unbelievable sight — she was dressed like a commoner, standing in the middle of a patch of dirt.

When I asked what exactly it was that she was doing…

"I am currently communicating with the origins of my magic: the earth. I felt that the fastest and most efficient way to do so was to till the earth and work the fields, and so that was what I did," Katarina responded, seemingly proud of the conclusion she had arrived at.

It was hilarious. I was ready to give it all up there and then and simply laugh in her face. Suppressing my laughter with great effort, I lifted my head, my gaze meeting with Katarina's. Her aqua-blue eyes stared straight into mine. Then I approached and knelt before her.

"Do you accept my proposal?"

"Oh… Um. Uh. Yes." Answering without much of a thought, Katarina's eyes told me all I needed to know — she was confused, verily so. The sight of her made me want to laugh all the more.

This young girl with brown hair and upwards-slanting, almond-shaped, aqua-blue eyes… For the first time in my life, I felt strongly drawn to another person.

Somehow, I had a feeling that my painfully boring life of being surrounded by equally boring individuals… was about to take a very different turn.

Several weeks after I formally accepted Prince Jeord's proposal, I answered a summons from my father. I walked over to see him after I finished my daily swordplay practice. Lately my family members had stopped recommending that I see a doctor, so I wondered what he wanted.

By the way, my tutor was full of praise for me again, as usual. "You have done most splendidly today, Lady Katarina. Excellent! Now, we just have to fix your footwork…" This was the kind of feedback I heard a lot.

It seemed that they were close to choosing a magic tutor for me, so that part of my plan was going smoothly too. At this rate, I would be able to dodge Jeord's attacks no problem, and maybe even build myself a magical business empire if I were exiled from the kingdom. I was definitely on my way towards defeating all of the Catastrophic Bad Ends.

I was in a good mood, humming cheerfully as I skipped all the way to my father's study. Little did I know that upon cheerfully entering the room, more Catastrophic Bad Ends awaited me, like assassins in the dark.

"Katarina, since you have become formally engaged to Prince Jeord, there is no one left to inherit the Claes name! To remedy this, I have decided to adopt a child from one of our branch families."

With those words, my smiling father held out his hand, and from behind his shadow came a small boy who looked to be my age. He seemed incredibly nervous — maybe he felt intimidated by the finery of the manor.

With a wave of his hand, my father introduced the mysterious boy. "This is Keith. From today, he will be your adopted little brother. Katarina, you are his older sister now. Please take good care of him."

Taking the cue, the boy approached me timidly. "...I'm Keith. I will be in your care..." he said, obviously not used to speaking so formally.

IT'S HERE! IT'S HEREEEEEE! The second Catastrophic Bad End Flag! With that, my previously upbeat mood was instantly destroyed.

While I knew this day would come, it felt a little too soon. Actually, it was *definitely* too soon. I'd hardly had time to come up with any contingency plans for Keith!

Keith Claes: Katarina's adopted brother, and one of the four possible love interests in *Fortune Lover*. In the game's setting, he was a flirtatious playboy.

Stunned by this development, I stood, speechless. My father, prompting me with some well-placed eye movements, reminded me that I hadn't introduced myself yet.

"K... Katarina. I'm Katarina. Nice to meet you."

In response to my fumbled greeting, Keith lowered his head once more. Now only a child of eight, he didn't seem at all like the character I knew from the game. For one, he wasn't flirtatious at all. Of course, we would have a huge problem on our hands if an eight-year-old did behave that way.

Even so, he was a cute and lovable-looking kid. Since he was one of the love interests, that made sense. Just looking at his flaxen, ever-so-slightly messy hair made me want to ruffle it obsessively. His blue eyes were so round — he was impossibly cute.

Come to think of it, I'd always wanted a little sister or brother in my previous life. I remembered asking my mom about it a bunch of times, only to be told coldly that it was "no longer possible." So I was overjoyed that I was now blessed with a little brother. I wanted to spoil him as much as I could.

Unfortunately, since Keith was a potential love interest of the protagonist, his very existence was a Catastrophic Bad Ending Flag for me. While I was happy to welcome a cute little brother into my life… the fact that he was a Bad Ending Flag traumatized me. *But he's… he's so cute… But… Ugh.* Either way, I decided that it was fine for me to be happy, for now.

"…. And so I ended up adopting him into this household. Katarina, Katarina… Were you listening to your father?"

"…Y-Yes father! Of course! I was listening!" When I came back to my senses, I realized that my father had been talking all this time. But I hadn't absorbed any of it.

"And so… Keith is tired from his long journey, as you can see. He will be resting for the day. Take good care of him from tomorrow on, understand?" My father was right — from Keith's expression alone, I could tell that he was exhausted.

And with that, Keith was gone, led away by my father to his new bedroom. After watching them disappear around a corner, I made a beeline for my room, hurrying as fast as I could. As soon as I got back, I retrieved the papers where I'd recorded the memories of my past life. I personally called it the "*Fortune Lover* Unofficial Strategy Guide."

Immediately after realizing that I was in the world of an otome game I had played before my death, I had written down as much information as possible. I turned to the page with the entry on Keith Claes.

Keith Claes.

A lonely, independent character. He was fathered by the patriarch of a Claes branch family, but his mother was a prostitute. At age three, he was taken into his father's care.

Due to his mother being a prostitute, Keith was frequently bullied by his older half-brothers. Once, when Keith was pushed to his limit after being bullied by them, his magical powers were awakened. His strong magic struck out at his cruel siblings and injured them. But this act made him even more of an outcast.

Duke Claes, having heard of Keith's magical prowess, decided to adopt him into the main family. However, the Claes family did not accept Keith as one of their own. His adoptive older sister, Katarina, who received all her father's attention up until then, came to hate her adopted brother. To make things worse, Duke Claes' wife jumped to the conclusion that Keith was the child of her husband's non-existent mistress, so she also stayed distant from him.

Faced with the potential wrath of Lady Katarina and Madam Claes, even the servants of the house were powerless to help him openly. Keith would spend most of his time alone, cooped up in his room. To cover up his childhood trauma and feelings of abandonment, Keith would become a womanizer and build up a terrible reputation.

After entering the academy, Keith would meet the protagonist, first approaching her with his flirtatious playboy façade. But then he'd eventually be drawn to the protagonist's gentle nature, her bright smile slowly healing the pain he had felt over the years. Before he knew it, he would become the charmed one. For the first time in his life, Keith realizes that he truly loves someone.

As expected, Katarina Claes plays a huge role in this route, living up to her villainous reputation. Enraged at the fact that the mere commoner protagonist had the gall to speak to someone from the Claes household, Katarina continually bullies Keith and his newfound love, all in the name of keeping the noble bloodlines pure.

And what awaited Katarina at the end of the Keith route was...

In the happy ending, the protagonist succeeds in romancing Keith. Much like Jeord's scenario, Katarina is stripped of her title and exiled from the kingdom for her continuous harassment of Keith and his love. Soon after, Keith would leave the Claes family, eloping with the protagonist.

In the bad ending, Keith fails to protect the protagonist from one of Katarina's ploys, and is severely injured and scarred in the process. Having sunk into the depths of despair, Keith summons up a powerful burst of magic, killing his sister in retaliation, before disappearing into the far corners of the lands.

Taking in all the relevant information, I sighed deeply. *How could this be? Why does Katarina Claes have no happy endings?! These are all terrible endings! In fact, the only thing that's different is how Katarina dies! By the sword or by magic... C'mon, she did her best as a villainess. How could she only have bad ends? This sucks!*

And so that's how "we" ended up holding yet another strategy meeting, determined to rise up from the ashes against yet another Catastrophic Bad End Flag.

Without further ado, let the second Katarina Claes Catastrophic Bad End Avoidance Strategy Meeting commence.

"Keeping with the trend established by our first meeting, I look forward to your great ideas, ladies."

"I have a suggestion."

"Yes. Well then, Lady Katarina Claes, if you would."

"This Catastrophic Bad Ending doesn't differ that much from Jeord's scenario. Could we not simply continue to hone our skills at the sword, and work towards establishing a magic-fueled business empire in the event of exile?"

"However... in this case, the sword has nothing to do with how Katarina is done in! If she is slain by magic, we will have to counter it with magic of our own!"

"But take into consideration that the enemy has strong magical powers. In fact, that was the entire reason why he was adopted into the family! Katarina, who can only use Dirt Bump, could never compare no matter how hard she worked!"

"Furthermore, the enemy is ever-present! He is under this very same roof. Letting our guard down for just a moment could be fatal!"

"N-No... How can that be? What should we do?! We've come this far, and even avoided Jeord's Catastrophic Bad End!"

"In this case... we have no choice. We'll... have to tie up loose ends."

"HM?! Do you mean...?!"

"I value my own life, you know. There's no choice..."

"No... That can't be!"

"You'll have to do it yourself. There's no other way. Although he is the cute little brother I've always wanted... nothing can be done! There is no other way! We have to stuff him into a box and throw him down the manor's longest flight of stairs!"

"N-No... I can't do something so cruel..."

"But there are no other solutions!"

"Um. Apologies for interrupting your heated discussion, but... if I may?"

"What is it, Lady Katarina Claes?! Do you have any better suggestions that could turn this entire thing around?!"

"...Yes. To be precise... Keith only fell for the protagonist because her presence healed his loneliness and pain. So... if Keith isn't lonely in the first place, he wouldn't fall for the protagonist, would he...?"

"Wha?!"

"And... if Keith doesn't fall for the protagonist, Katarina Claes wouldn't face a Catastrophic Bad End!"

"Wh-What insight! What wisdom! Katarina Claes, you are a GENIUS!"

"Yes! That's exactly it! This is wonderful!"

"Well then, all we have to do is ensure that Keith isn't lonely. Is that the battle plan?"

"Yes, of course. However... how exactly would we ensure that he isn't lonely?"

"Hmm. How about we never leave him to his own devices... and just spoil him, and stay by his side often?"

"Well, that's simple enough. All we have to do is shower our brother with love! So to summarize... We just have to do what we wanted to do in the first place! How delightful!"

"Well then, with this, I declare that the appropriate way to disarm the Keith Claes Catastrophic Bad End Flag will be to simply shower him with sisterly love."

"Agreed."

"Agreed."

And with this, the second Katarina Claes Catastrophic Bad End Avoidance Strategy Meeting came to an end.

"So all I have to do is love my adopted little brother!" This was too amazing for me to believe. "I'll invite him out to play tomorrow..." And with that, I promptly fell asleep.

I did, however, forget one important detail... In *Fortune Lover*, even Katarina's mother picked on Keith, eventually contributing to his suffering and loneliness.

The next day, we were both seated at the breakfast table. Keith seemed somewhat recovered from his journey after a night's worth of rest. Not wanting to pass up this opportunity, I immediately invited Keith out to play.

"The weather today is delightful — I'll show you around the garden, Keith. You must not have seen it, given how you went to bed straight away last night."

"Y-Yes. Thank you very much, Lady Katarina," Keith said, acknowledging my words formally. My own brother, treating me like a stranger! I puffed out my cheeks in defiance.

"Keith, we are brother and sister, you know. You should call me Big Sister! Also, you can drop the formalities with me."

"But then, would that not be rude of me..." Keith said, somewhat wary of my suggestion.

"Ugh, we're siblings, Keith! It's fine! Also, I've always wanted a younger sibling to call me Big Sister. It's one of my many dreams! Please, don't be afraid to call me that!" I said, my face now dangerously close to Keith's. In my excitement, I forgot to monitor my behavior — Keith now looked taken aback, and was shrinking into his seat.

Then, at my passionate request, Keith finally called me "Big Sister." *Oh, cute little brother of mine. This is pure bliss.*

With that, I pulled Keith behind me as I ran out of the manor and into the garden. The clear blue sky and good weather made it a perfect day for a walk. As expected for a duke's manor, it was pointlessly and impossibly large. In fact, a small stream ran through the grounds, complete with the obligatory pond.

"There are fish in this stream, Keith! We can fish here."

"…Fish…?" Keith, who had been peeking out at the stream from behind me, seemed surprised.

"Yes, fishing! Have you never done it before?"

"…No, I have not…"

"I'm pretty good at it, you know? We should try it together next time!"

"You have… fished before?"

"I have! And I'll teach you how, Keith," I said, nodding proudly. This only made Keith look even more surprised. Actually he'd seemed that way for a while now.

While I hadn't gone fishing yet since becoming Katarina, I did fish up basketfuls of carp and crayfish in my previous life. So I was completely confident that I'd be able to do the same in this life.

Next, I led Keith to the fields. Ever since my first encounter with Prince Jeord, I had gotten a lot of assistance from the gardeners and servants with my little project, and small sprouts of various vegetables now peeked out of the tilled dirt.

"This over here is an eggplant… And there are the tomatoes," I said, pointing out the crops to Keith. It seemed that the vegetables in this world were pretty much the same as those from in my previous life.

"…Fields? Did you… plant these vegetables, Big Sister?"

"Yes, I did! In the beginning I was doing it myself, but I guess it's a little difficult for a complete amateur. Now, the gardeners and servants help me with it. I promised that we would hold a party and cook up a storm after the harvest. Make sure you have some too, Keith."

At my words, Keith's expression of surprise seemed to have reached its zenith. He had been like this all day. Looking at Keith's cute face and perpetually open, gaping-in-surprise mouth, I couldn't help but compare it to his original character: the Keith who had spent all his childhood cooped up alone in his room. He probably never really had the chance to play outside, let alone see anything like this. I wanted to show more and more things to him.

"Keith... I'll show you my favorite place next!" I grabbed his hand once more, leading him away in a flurry of footsteps.

"Here it is!" I said, pointing to a large tree on the outskirts of the garden. It was the largest tree on the family manor's grounds, and was definitely my favorite. I often read books under it, or took naps in the shade. But more than anything else...

"The view from up there is the best!"

As I said, the scenery you could see from the top of the garden's tallest tree was spectacular. According to my memories, Katarina wasn't very interested in climbing trees. I, on the other hand, was once known as a wild monkey for my tree-climbing tendencies. Naturally, I was excited to climb such a tall tree.

In fact, I had marked this tree for climbing from the moment I saw it, and eventually managed to make it all the way to the top during breaks from field work.

"You're... climbing it...?"

"Yes, tree climbing! Have you climbed a tree before?"

Keith, with his mouth still open wide and gaping, shook his head in response. *That would be a no, I suppose.*

"Well then! I will teach you all I know. First, watch my movements…"

With that, I took off my shoes and tossed them carelessly to one side. After hiking up my dress, I latched onto the tree's trunk and began climbing it.

Although the dress hampered my movements more than my typical gardening overalls did, that wasn't nearly enough to stop me — before long, I had made good progress. Such was the power of one who was known as the wild monkey of the back hills. Though my tree-climbing had apparently embarrassed my family, and they pleaded with me many times to stop.

I continued my ascent. Now used to moving in the dress, my mind became focused, and my speed increased as I climbed. Faster and faster I went. The genius of tree climbing, the wild monkey… I had many names, but I did have one flaw…

And that was getting a little too ahead of myself. My parents, and even my teachers often warned me not to bite off more than I could chew — in fact, this was the reason why I'd passed on from my previous life in the first place. Even after dying once and having been reborn, I unfortunately still had that same flaw. *I suppose old habits die hard.*

Having reached the middle of the tree, I turned, waving to Keith at the bottom with a beaming smile on my face. I wasn't thinking about safety at all. Feeling invincible, I waved even harder. Predictably, this made me lose balance and fall completely off the tree.

As I fell down onto the garden grounds in what felt like slow motion, my previous family's parting words echoed in my mind. *"You idiot…!"*

With a tremendous thud, I landed bottom-first on the ground. I braced myself, knowing that it was impossible for me not to injure myself falling from so high. *But... Hmm? It doesn't hurt very much at all. Am I that sturdy? In fact, it feels like I landed on something soft...*

I turned my gaze downwards. "K-Keith?!"

Since when did my cute little brother become a soft cushion for me to sit on?! In fact, why does it look like I landed on him bottom-first, and why is he sprawled out on the ground like that?!

"Noooo! Keith... Don't die, Keith...! Oh no, my poor, cute little brother!" Hugging Keith's sprawled-out body, I started bawling my lungs out.

Is this divine punishment for me thinking about throwing him down the stairs in a box last night? No... it can't be. I've killed my new brother with my own butt!

My crying intensified as I howled out Keith's name. "KEEEEEITH! DON'T DIE!"

"Um... Big Sister?"

"Don't die... Who... Who could have known? How could this be? How could I kill my brother with my butt?! Keith...!"

"Um... are you listening to me, Big Sister?"

"Don't dieeeee!! KEEEEEITHHH!"

"Big Sister KATARINA!!"

A sudden loud voice snapped me out of my grief. Looking up from the body that I had been hugging, I came face to face with Keith, his eyes now wide open. For a moment, our blue eyes met, and confusion and relief stirred in my chest.

"Keith?! Y... YOU'RE ALIVE!" Overcome with emotion, I hugged Keith even harder. My brother, however, suddenly became rigid in my arms.

"Wha— Does it hurt somewhere?"

"…I am alright. I just… fell on my back. Just a small impact to the back. I'm fine," Keith said with a faint smile.

He doesn't look fine to me at all! He must be pretending to be alright for my sake…!

"Wait here, Keith. I'll get some help and bring you back to the manor right away."

Since I had been a commoner in my last life, I wasn't exactly used to having an entourage, and so I had dismissed my servants before setting out. And now, something terrible had happened without them here…!

Reassuring Keith despite my own panicked expression, I turned and ran as fast as I could to the manor.

Fortunately, Keith only ended up with a bruise. According to the doctor, he would recover in no time.

As I prostrated myself before my brother in genuine remorse, Keith, the angel he was, just said, "I am glad you are unhurt, Big Sister."

Moved by his gentle nature, I started bawling my heart out again. With that, I was forgiven by Keith, and was cautioned by my father and the servants to be more careful as I was out and about. And so, my adventure was over… Or so I thought.

After finishing my dinner, I retreated to my room, ready to roll straight into bed. But before I could, I received a summons from my mother.

Honestly, I'd been trying to avoid her as much as possible ever since the engagement with Jeord. I wondered what she wanted me for. In any case, I allowed Anne to tidy up my hair as much as she could, and then made my way to my mother's chambers.

On my way to her room, I suddenly remembered a certain detail from *Fortune Lover*. *Come to think of it… in the setting of the game, Katarina's mother, Madam Claes, also gave Keith a really hard time, due to thinking that he was the child of her husband's mistress.*

Yes, now I remember — I heard rumors like that circulating amongst the servants when Keith was first brought here, probably because of his blue eyes, which look like my father's. It doesn't help that the marriage between Madam Milidiana Claes and my father, Duke Luigi Claes, was more political than romantic… which is pretty common in the world of nobles.

While my father was a daughter-obsessed, somewhat jovial middle-aged man now, he had been quite the playboy in the past, and had no shortage of female suitors who were lining up in hopes of becoming his bride.

Milidiana Adiss was the second daughter of the Adiss family, which happened to be of similar social standing to the Claes family. With her upwards-slanting, almond-shaped eyes and her shy demeanor, however, few suitors seemed interested in her.

At the recommendation of Duke Adiss, it was decided that their families would be united, with Luigi taking Milidiana as his bride… And that was the abridged history of my parents' marriage.

On the surface the two didn't seem to fight or argue, but even Katarina, their daughter, could see that her parents were aloof with one another. This was why Keith was assumed to be my father's illegitimate child, given the similarity of their eyes. This was the rumor that was now circulating amongst the servants. Well actually, since earlier today they'd had something else to talk about: "The young miss has done it again," due to my tree-climbing misadventure…

Despite what everyone thought, I had the knowledge from the game and knew full well that Keith was no illegitimate child. But my mother didn't have that privilege. For both their sakes, I had to make sure that they knew the truth.

At that moment, my thoughts were interrupted by a set of imposing doors. We had arrived at my mother's chambers. Upon entering the room, I was surprised to see my father and Keith there as well.

Wh-What is this? I had no clue what was going on. I looked pointedly at my father for an explanation only for him to glance back absentmindedly, as if he didn't know what was happening either. Keith, of course, knew even less than we did. He just stood there awkwardly in the unnecessarily large room.

Finally deciding to break the strange atmosphere, Mother began to speak. "My dear husband, Katarina, Keith… I have an important request to make," she said with an expression of deep sorrow.

"What is this all of a sudden, Milidiana?" Father's expression hardened as he gazed at my mother's pained face.

Mother lowered her head in the general direction of his gaze. Then she said, "Please divorce me, my dear husband, and live happily ever after."

"…"

Complete silence filled the room after this sudden statement — I, my father, Keith, and even the servants collectively held our breaths.

Mother continued, disregarding our shocked faces. "To take an unwanted woman such as myself as your bride was one thing… But look! Even the single daughter born of my body has turned out to be such a terrible child! To think that she has even injured your precious son, Keith... I deeply apologize for her actions. I will take this hopeless daughter back with me to the Adiss manor... I only pray that you, my dear husband, will live a happy life with Keith and his mother."

Having finally said those words, tears streamed down my mother's face. In other words, she wished to be divorced from my father so he could live happily ever after with Keith's mother, this supposed lover who actually didn't exist. She didn't know that, of course.

But, like, my own mother called me hopeless in front of everybody... *Hmm, well I guess my parents in my previous life were always saying the same thing.*

The atmosphere in the room was now completely frozen, with everyone acting like they'd been petrified by a cold wind. For a while, no one spoke.

The first one to break that silence was my father. "What are you saying, my dear Milidiana? To begin with, who is this... mother of Keith, that you speak of?"

"You don't have to hide it! I know that he is the child of you and your mistress. This... *wife* that you took in the name of a political marriage will disappear with her hopeless daughter. I only pray that you live a long, happy life with your new lover... So there you have it. Katarina, Pack your things."

Mother wailed, tears continuing to fall from her bloodshot eyes. She looked like she wanted to flee the house as soon as possible... And she would even take her "hopeless daughter" along!

While I did understand how my mother was feeling, I never knew that she was this desperate. It seemed like the "I fell from a tree and landed on Keith!" incident had caused a floodgate within her mind to burst open.

Will they really divorce each other just like that? Yet another collective silence fell over the room. All the servants and I could do was watch.

My father, having moved to my mother's side at some point in time, slowly put a hand on her quivering shoulder. He had a sad expression on his face too, as if he was also ready to cry at any moment. Of course he would react in this way — he had just been accused of adultery, and was now about to be divorced. It would have been stranger if he wasn't upset.

"...My dear..." Mother looked up at him, her eyes seemingly ready to melt from the sheer amount of tears they were shedding.

"Oh, Milidiana... All the time we've been married, I could see in your eyes that there was something dividing us. I had assumed that it was because we had gotten married without your permission and blessing — that you have never found it in your heart to forgive me."

"...Well, no... that was because you had many other brides to pick from, my dear husband. The only reason you chose me was to improve the relations between our families, was it not? Because of your obligations towards Duke Adiss? You had no choice in the matter, and I always... regretted that..."

At the end of my mother's monologue, my father suddenly hugged her tightly. *Eh...? What was this sudden development?* The entire room, as confused and surprised as I was, still watched on silently.

"Oh, my dear Milidiana... So that was what you thought all along? I am so sorry... to not have made clear my true feelings. Because of that... I have caused you so much pain. Milidiana... allow me to say it again. I love you."

"...M-My dear..."

"When Duke Adiss first introduced me to you, I fell for you there and then... When I heard that the Duke had not decided on a potential engagement for you, I was elated! Beside myself! I decided that I had to make you mine under any circumstances... And so I rushed the entire affair. After that, you always avoided me... I thought that you hated me for what I had done, for forcing you to marry me!"

"...No... In fact, I, too, fell for you the moment I saw you... But I thought that you were just taking me for political reasons, and that you actually disliked me..."

"Oh, Milidiana... It would seem that we have both misunderstood each other."

"My dear husband...!"

And with that, the carnage of divorce was averted, instead replaced by a dramatic scene of true love. Judging by the smitten expressions on their faces, my parents now only had eyes for each other.

Everyone else who had been watching all this time could only look on, bewildered, as my parents' touching scene of rekindled love played before our eyes.

"Young miss, young master. It is almost bedtime. Let us return to your rooms..." one of our loyal servants said before shepherding us out of my mother's chambers.

The other servants left with us. I could tell that the world within the doors that closed behind us was now strictly reserved for the Claes couple. We stood outside the room as the servants filed out, then were eventually led back to our rooms.

Before I went to bed, I wished Keith goodnight, thanking him for his patience through all of this. Keith responded the same way, though with a troubled expression on his face.

"Goodnight, Big Sister," Keith said as he retreated to his room.

Hmm. So much ado about nothing.

Now that I think about it, my father often tells me my villainess-like face is angelic. Specifically, he calls me his "cutest angel." I look like my mother, so he must think that this face we share is beautiful. In contrast, my father was just flat-out handsome in the most classic sense, but to each their own.

With this, the misunderstandings surrounding Keith were over, and my mother no longer thought of him as an illegitimate child. She would treat him kindly from now on. The entire situation was wrapped up, without any more unpleasant surprises.

With that, the sun finally set on one of the most tiringly long days of my life.

A few weeks had passed since the "Katarina fell out of a tree and nearly flattened her new brother" and "the Claes couple's divorce crisis" incidents.

Since then, the days had passed peacefully. I had finally been assigned a magic tutor, and I would start seriously training my magical skills soon. Keith had gradually become used to the household, and had grown much closer to me.

The only problem I was having was the black-hearted Prince Jeord showing up at the manor on a regular basis since our engagement. He had apparently somehow heard about my tree misadventure, and turned up to make sure I was okay. I wasn't injured to a point where I needed visitors, so I calmly explained to Jeord that Keith had cushioned my fall, and I was completely fine.

How embarrassing, given that I was called the "wild monkey" in my past life! In what world do monkeys fall from trees? Well, at least the only reason I'd fallen was because I wasn't paying attention, not because of my tree-climbing skills.

I found myself passionately describing the chain of events to the prince. But for some reason his shoulders started shaking as I got to the good part, and I couldn't tell if he was actually listening to me or not.

On another subject, my parents, having overcome the trauma of the "the Claes couple's divorce crisis" incident, had become impossibly lovey-dovey. It was super embarrassing. I started thinking pretty often that the two should get a room, or better yet, a new world for themselves. At this rate, I was in store for another brother or sister. *Honestly, I really wish they'd calm down.*

In fact, my mother, who had been so cold and cruel to Keith in the game, had now changed her whole attitude. Maybe it was because of her newfound love with my father. All she had to say about Keith was how he would be, "beautiful and dashing when he grows up, just like your father!" In fact, she spoiled him regularly, while ignoring me, her actual daughter...

Even my father's catch phrase changed! He now says "Katarina, you are exactly like Milidiana! The cutest in the world!" all the time.

And so, the originally fractured and sorrowful Claes family of the game had now evolved into a warm and loving one.

One day after finishing our swordplay practice, Keith and I visited the fields in the garden. On top of his gentle personality, my cute little brother was really talented at the sword, and was praised by our tutor today.

I felt very proud of him, as any good big sister should. I also got more praise from our tutor on my constantly improving swordplay, though there was still apparently an issue with my footwork.

The crops were growing steadily, getting bigger with each passing day.

"I never asked, Big Sister, but why are you tending to these fields in the first place?" Keith asked, staring at a sprouting cucumber plant.

"Oh, right. I guess I never did tell you about it."

I told Keith about how I'd originally wanted to communicate with the origin of my magic, the earth. But I'd forgotten that plan a long time ago, and now I was raising the crops as a hobby.

"...Tilling the earth and working the fields to... communicate with one's point of origin and improve one's magic? Something about that... is off..." That was what Keith said as he heard my response, muttering to himself as he gasped and gaped.

Hmm. Haven't I heard this somewhere before? Maybe I'm misremembering things.

"Come to think of it, you have strong magical power, right? What exactly can you do?"

Keith was, after all, adopted into the Claes family in part due to his magical abilities. I was sure he could do spells that were more impressive than my Dirt Bump.

Although I had turned to Keith with a beaming, expectant expression, I was surprised to find that he looked apprehensive, his features hardening.

"Hm...? Keith? What's wrong?"

"It's nothing," Keith said, slowly shaking his head.

"Oh? Well see... I can't do anything but this!" With that, I showed Keith my secret hidden technique: Katarina Claes' Dirt Bump.

A smile returned to Keith's face. "It's... tiny."

"Yes, you see! It's tiny! Honestly! I wish I could make a wall of earth, or maybe an Earth Golem and move it around..." I hung my head, disappointed by my own abilities.

Keith stood in place, repeating a single phrase. "Earth... Golem?"

"Yes! I'd like to try controlling an Earth Golem!"

If I remembered right, Keith could control golems made of earth, which he used to help the protagonist at various points of the story. Remembering that particular scene, an idea crossed my mind. If I could control an Earth Golem myself, I could make it do whatever I wanted. *A golem doesn't need any pay, so I could make a good amount of coin! In fact, with this ability, I could easily survive outside the kingdom even if I were exiled! I'd just command the golem to build up an empire of riches for me.*

"I tried to make one before, but I don't really know how. That's right! You can do it, can't you Keith?" I would be surprised if he couldn't, since it was the same magic he used in the game.

"...Well... I suppose. But..."

"Please, Keith! A little bit is fine! Show me! Show me!"

Although Keith seemed hesitant, I continued begging him, asking him to just show me a tiny bit of his magic.

"...All right then, but only a little..." he said finally, nodding.

"Yay! Thank you very much, Keith!"

YES! I'VE DONE IT! With this, I'll earn tons of coin with my magic! I'll avoid the Catastrophic Bad End! I might even establish the Katarina Corporation! I was so happy that I did a little jig on the spot.

Apparently, Keith had played with dolls made of earth when living in his previous home. After his abilities had awakened, his magic had crept into these dolls and made them move. In order to show me this power, Keith crafted a small golem of about ten centimeters tall from the garden soil. My new brother was even good with his hands!

After he finished making it, Keith placed his hands on his creation and slowly closed his eyes. After a while, he opened them — and the golem started walking about, in small but steady steps.

"Th-That's amazing, Keith! It's moving! The golem is moving!"

"If I infuse some of my magic into the Earth Golem, I can make it move as I please…" Keith explained as I continued celebrating noisily.

"Hey, Keith! Are they all of this size?" The golem that had carried the protagonist around in the game I'd played was much, much bigger.

"If I infuse even more magic into the golem, it'll become bigger… Would you like to see?"

Keith had a somewhat conflicted expression as I looked on, my sparkling eyes filled with expectation. I nodded vigorously. After all, what could I do with a ten-centimeter golem? I would need a much, much bigger golem to expand the scope of my business.

Keith's expression darkened somewhat, but, maybe not wanting to disappoint me when I was so eager and expectant, he placed his hands on the golem again. Almost immediately the previously ten-centimeter golem erupted in size, and was now standing at almost three meters tall.

I gave a loud, spirited cheer. "Wow! That's really impressive, Keith! You're a genius! Hey, hey Keith! Can you move this golem around like the small one just now?" I asked wildly.

"…Yes, it can move in a similar way."

"Please! Move it! Move it!"

"…Well, just a little…" And with that, the three-meter tall Earth Golem started moving, its steps resounding in loud thuds.

This is it! I finally felt like I was really in a magical kingdom. Honestly, up until now I hadn't seen any magic besides my unfortunate Dirt Bump. And calling that spell "magic" was a little sad.

Magic didn't exist in my previous world, but I wished it did. In fact, I often wondered if things would be different if I were able to use magic.

And now… this is real magic, before my very eyes. I wanted to touch it, to feel that walking, magic-powered golem with my hands. With that thought in mind, I slowly approached the walking golem.

Keith, who had been controlling the golem from somewhere behind where I was standing, seemed to have muttered something. I was having too much fun to listen. I approached the golem slowly, stretching out my hand. Unfortunately, that was when the three-meter-tall golem's arm began to move.

The golem's giant arm hit me, probably on my chest, much more strongly than I had realized at first. My small body was launched up and away, soaring through the air, before coming to an abrupt landing head-first on the cold, hard ground.

How unlucky can a girl get? Everything seems to go wrong for me!

From the depths of my rapidly-fading consciousness, I could hear Keith's voice, repeatedly calling out to me.

Ah, there's my cute brother, worrying about me again… I'm sorry, Keith.

Then, everything faded to black.

When I woke up, I was lying on the bed in my room. There was a middle-aged man, his face covered in snot and tears. It was the face of my father.

"Katarina! You... You're awake!" my father exclaimed, hugging me tight.

The force of the hug sent a dull, throbbing ache through my body. A lot of his snot and tears ended up all over me. *Please... not the face.* I was trying to wrestle my way out of his embrace when my mother walked into the room.

"Katarina, now that you are awake, how do you feel?" she asked.

"How do I... feel?"

"Do you not remember? You were launched into the air by the golem that Keith made, and then hit your head on the ground. You were unconscious."

"...Ah! That's right!" My attempts to dodge my father's snot had made me forget why I was in bed in the first place.

Even my mother, who had been spending most of her time fussing over Keith lately, seemed genuinely worried. "Well? How do you feel? We had a doctor come by and look at your head, but other than a swollen bump and a bit of swelling on your back, you should be fine."

"Hmm... My head does hurt a little. Ah, there really is a bump..." I said, feeling the injury on my head with my fingers. There was also a slight, throbbing pain in my back.

"In any case, the doctor has said that you will heal in a few weeks. Until then, be sure you rest in peace and quiet. You are prohibited from going out into the gardens until you have recovered."

"Huuuh? But I have to take care of the fiiields...!"

My protest was immediately answered by a chilling glare from my mother. "If you don't listen, Katarina Claes, I will see to it that you are forbidden from ever entering the gardens again from here on out."

"N-No... Not that..."

"Until you are better, you are not to venture into the gardens. You will stay here and behave yourself, young lady. Do you understand?!"

"...Yes, Mother." I retreated into my bed, like a frog caught in a snake's predatory gaze. "Hey... Anne?" I whispered softly to my personal maidservant, Anne, who had been standing next to me the whole time.

"What is it, young miss?"

"Maybe I'm wrong, but from what I remember... isn't Mother usually a lot calmer than this?"

"Yes, I would suppose so. The madam has always been a calmer sort of person."

"See? I knew it. When did she become so forceful? Has she gotten more confidence because of her lovey-dovey stuff with Father?"

"...Young miss, I believe that a problematic child would cause a once-calm mother to become more... vigorous, if I may say so. After all, parents do change for their children's sakes..."

"What do you mean, problematic child? Keith is a very well-behaved little brother!"

"...I really cannot begin to imagine the depths of madam's sorrow..." Anne said, before shaking her head and muttering incoherently to herself.

"Oh, right! What about Keith? Is Keith okay?" I asked, raising my voice unintentionally.

My father, who had been mumbling "Thank God Katarina is alright...!" to himself all this time, blew his nose unceremoniously before answering my question. "Keith returned to his room after the doctor announced that you were alright."

61

"Oh, really? Keith kept calling my name when I got injured... He must be worried sick about me!"

"Katarina... On the matter of Keith..." My father's expression suddenly became serious, which was very different from his usual dopey self.

"What is it, Father?"

"Well. Keith... has strong magical aptitude, but he cannot yet control his powers. This was why we employed a magic tutor, and Keith promised that he would not carelessly use his powers until he had learned how to control them. I believe I explained this to you when you first met Keith, Katarina."

"...N-No..." *What does he mean? I don't remember hearing anything... Oh, right! He was saying something when I first met Keith... but I was too lost in my own thoughts to listen.* "I am very sorry, Father. I did not hear a single word you said..."

"Well... I thought that might have been the case," my father said, a slightly defeated smile on his face. Mother, who had been listening in from the sidelines, had an exasperated expression on her face.

"I did not speak of this to you, but... Keith had once injured his siblings in his previous abode. He lost control of his magical powers, you see. Keith is very afraid of his abilities potentially hurting someone... So I was surprised to hear that he had used magic at all."

I remembered how Keith had reacted when I asked him to show me his magic. I was too busy drowning in my own excitement at the time, but now I could see that my request made him nervous. He had hesitated a lot before showing his magic to me.

"Keith also said... 'I broke my promise to not use magic, and I also hurt my big sister. It's all my fault, so I will accept any punishment.'"

"What?! No! This wasn't Keith's fault! I asked him to show me—No, I pestered him to do it! Also..."

In fact... when I went up to the golem, Keith did try to warn me. I just didn't listen because I was too excited. I remember hearing something like, "Stop! It's dangerous, Big Sister! Don't go any closer!"

"Keith also warned me not to approach the golem... But I was so excited to see the magic that I didn't listen. Keith isn't to blame! It's all my fault for getting carried away. I'm really sorry..." I lowered my head in remorse, apologizing repeatedly to Father, Mother, and even Anne, who had been worried about me all this time. "So... If there is going to be any punishment, I would like to be responsible and take it all myself," I said, looking up at my father.

"Thank you for telling us the truth, my dear Katarina. I have no intention of punishing either you or Keith. However, it is also true that you have been a little too reckless lately. You have to rest until you are better — do you understand?" my father said, gently patting me on the head.

Mother mumbled to herself, saying something along the lines of "...I would hardly call her just 'a little reckless'..."

"I have to apologize properly to Keith..."

"Yes, you should. But it is already late today. You can do it tomorrow, Katarina," said Father as he looked out the window.

It was already pitch black — I guess the sun had set a long time ago. It was noon when I went outside with Keith, so that meant I had been asleep for almost half a day.

"Well... I'll go apologize tomorrow, then."

"Yes, that is for the best. And do be more careful from now on..." Father patted my head once more before leaving my room with Mother in tow.

After helping me get ready for bed, Anne tucked me in and wished me goodnight. Keith's face floated into my mind as soon as I closed my eyes. Although I hadn't paid much attention to what my father had said back then, I knew from my memories of the game that after Keith injured his brothers with his magic, he'd become even more isolated in his previous home.

Before I passed out, Keith had been calling out my name over and over, his voice sounding like a sorrowful wail. *What a terrible thing I've done...* I would definitely visit him early in the morning and apologize. Swearing upon my name to do just that, I closed my eyes and finally fell asleep.

But my vow was broken quickly, because Keith wouldn't come out of his room the next morning.

The day after I was sent flying by the Earth Golem, I made a beeline for Keith's room, planning to apologize. I knocked on his door, but no one answered. Maybe he wasn't awake yet?

If he really was sleeping, I would feel bad for disturbing him. Either way, I figured that Keith would show up at the breakfast table... but I was soon proven wrong. With the seat next to me empty, it was clear that Keith had decided to skip breakfast. Even my parents seemed worried.

Mother quickly leaned forward with a suspicious look on her face. "Katarina... what did you do to Keith when you visited his room early this morning?"

Rude! I haven't done anything yet!

But I was starting to feel worried, so after breakfast I immediately headed back to Keith's room and knocked on his door rapidly like I had that morning. Still hearing no response, I called out to Keith through the door instead.

"Keith! It's me, Katarina! You weren't at breakfast... Are you feeling okay?"

At that, a weak voice responded to me from beyond the door. "Big Sister..."

"Yes, it's me. What's wrong? Does your stomach hurt? Are you okay?"

"...Nothing is wrong... More importantly, how are your injuries, Big Sister?"

"I'm fine, it was just a little bump on the head! It doesn't matter. Keith... I'd like to speak to you. May I come in?" I was determined to apologize for what had happened yesterday. However...

"I'm sorry. I cannot let you in." Keith's responded with a firm rejection.

"Wh... Why?"

"...I can no longer be by your side, Big Sister."

After that, no more sound came from Keith's room. *What is going on? Does he suddenly not like me anymore?* Whatever the reason was, I wasn't going to find out by waiting around at the door. I put my hand on the knob and gave it a good turn, but it was locked.

No matter how many times I called out to Keith to open the door, there was no response. *What should I do?* If this went on, Keith would hate me, and remain confined in his room...

Confinement » loneliness » goes to the academy lonely and sad » is healed by the protagonist when he meets her eventually » loves the protagonist » Katarina becomes an obstacle » Katarina is exiled or killed by magic.

This is bad! This is really, really bad! This is now a straight line towards a Catastrophic Bad End!

Feeling desperate, I tried as hard as I could to pry open the door. But my efforts were interrupted by Anne's voice calling out to me.

"Young miss… What exactly are you doing?"

"Keith locked himself in and won't let me see him!"

"Well… Perhaps Keith would prefer that you do not enter," Anne said, her eyes focused on me in a calm, sympathetic gaze.

"Ugh, I guess that might be true. But he sounds strange! He isn't himself, Anne!" I was frantic.

"In that case, if you would really like to enter, there is a spare key in the servants' room… Young miss!"

As soon as those words had left Anne's lips, I made a mad dash to the servants' room. But to my dismay, Keith seemed to have thought ahead and taken the spare key before locking himself in.

You're too clever, Keith. But now I realized that my brother was determined to shut himself in. *This is bad! Really bad! If this is how it's going to be, I have no choice. Desperate times call for desperate measures.*

I ran somewhere, picked up something, and returned to Keith's door.

"Oh, young miss. Have you found the ke— What is that, young miss?! What exactly are you planning on doing?!" Anne, who had been waiting for me outside of Keith's room, raised her voice in alarm when she saw me.

Panting like a maniac, I replied, "I am opening the door. If Keith gets shut in like this, a disaster will happen!"

"You're opening the door with *that*? H-How? Are you going to… break it down? Let's calm down, young miss. Please put that thing down."

Anne tried desperately to stop me, but I was already past the point of no return. There was no other way. After all, if I just sat around and let this happen, the Catastrophic Bad End that I'd tried so hard to avoid would definitely come for me.

"Keith, step back from the door," I said loudly.

And then, with a deep breath, I raised the axe that I had retrieved from the garden storage shed over my head and swung it down onto the door.

"*Young miss!*"

The sound of metal on splintering wood, mixed with Anne's alarmed cries, echoed through the Claes family manor.

Having finally destroyed the door, I stepped into the room. Keith was sitting on his bed, staring at the doorway in shock, probably completely confused. Behind me, it sounded like Anne had run off, screaming to alert the household to the situation.

Well, I'll deal with the door later, I have to apologize.

"...Big Sister..." His eyes open in a familiar gaping expression, Keith seemed frozen to the spot as I walked towards him.

"I'm sorry about yesterday!" I said. Feeling like words weren't enough to express my regret, I got on my knees and pressed my head firmly to the floor in apology. "I'm really sorry for making you use your magic, and for being so pushy! And for not listening to your warnings about going near the golem! I'm so so sorry for worrying you!"

Before I knew it, Keith was kneeling down next to me, his voice shaking. "...Why are you apologizing, Big Sister...? I am the one at fault..."

"What are you talking about?! I am the one who was wrong! I asked you to do something you didn't want to do, Keith!"

My brother hung his head and spoke with a strained voice, as if something was squeezing his heart. "...Are you not... afraid of me, Big Sister?"

"Afraid?" *What does he mean?*

Well yeah, I'd be scared to death if this was the Keith who'd fallen in love with the protagonist and was pushing me towards a Catastrophic Bad End. Does Keith already hate me so much that he wants to get rid of me?! Have I already reached the bad ending I've been trying to avoid?!

"…In my previous home, I ended up hurting my brothers with my magic. This time, I hurt you, Big Sister. Although my magic is strong, I can't control it at all…"

I gulped fearfully. *So he does hate me for forcing him to use his magic…! Is it coming? The Catastrophic Bad End? Which is it?!*

"…I always end up losing control and hurting people… Even so, are you not afraid of me, Big Sister?"

"…Huh?" His voice wasn't enraged or hateful. *This isn't a bad ending?* "Ohh, that's what you meant!" I sighed deeply in relief.

Keith, who had been hanging his head, suddenly looked up at me in confusion. My eyes met with his beautiful blue ones.

"If you can't control your magic, you just have to keep practicing, right?"

I remembered that Keith was able to control his powerful magic just fine in the game. Right now, he was only eight years old. I was sure he'd learn to control it by the time he went to the academy.

"We'll have a magic tutor soon. We can practice together!" I said with a glowing smile full of relief.

At that, Keith, who had been quiet up until now, suddenly spoke. "…We can stay together, Big Sister?"

"Of course! I'll stay with you forever! Unless you don't like me anymore?"

Keith shook his head emphatically. It seemed that he didn't hate me after all. *Thank goodness.*

"So, even if something bad happens again, you can't lock yourself in your room— Keith! What is it?!" I had finally calmed down just a few moments ago, but now I was alarmed again as I saw tears rolling down from Keith's blue eyes. "Keith, what is it?! Are you hurt?!"

I panicked at the sight of the suddenly crying Keith. *Weren't we just talking normally? What have I done now?!* Although I continued to desperately pat him on the back, Keith wouldn't stop crying.

As Keith continued bawling, I could only sit next to him in a daze, not knowing what to do.

"…Katarina, what on earth have you done?"

I heard a low, almost gravelly voice from the entrance of Keith's room. Turning around, I saw none other than my mother, her features contorted in an almost demonic rage.

"Katarina, do you not remember how you promised you would rest quietly in your room until you were recovered, just yesterday…? What exactly has happened to this room? You even made your brother cry… What exactly is going on in that head of yours?"

"Ah… Um. Mother, this is…" I felt my blood freeze in my veins as if I had been lowered into a cage filled with circling lions.

"Katarina. Come to my room."

"…Eek!"

After grabbing me by the collar, Mother started consoling my brother soothingly. "Oh my dear Keith. You must have been so frightened. Don't worry, I will take *this one* away from you. Everything is alright now." Then she turned to me with an expression that could only be described as the polar opposite of soothing.

"...M-Mother. Wait. This is..." Although Keith himself tried to raise his head and say something in my defense, he had cried a little too much and couldn't find the words.

Before I realized what was happening, a wall of servants had assembled outside Keith's room. But unfortunately my father, who loved his daughter more than anything else in the world, wasn't with them.

And that was how I ended up being forcibly removed and dragged to my mother's chambers. With no allies to defend me, I ended up enduring a punishment in the form of a several-hour long lecture from my demonic mother.

When I was finally released from my torment a few hours later, I made my way back to my room, feeling completely drained. Anne already had a pot of tea ready for me, and her thoughtfulness soothed my heart. *I guess I should forgive her for reporting the axe incident to Mother.*

I drank deeply from the cup, heaving a final sigh. *Come to think of it, is Keith okay? He was crying a lot.* I turned to Anne, hoping for answers.

"After a while, he seemed to have calmed down."

"Really? That's good. But why was he crying like that?"

"...With all due respect, young miss, given that you suddenly destroyed a previously locked door with an axe in your hands, before approaching the person within while still holding the weapon... How did you think Keith would react?"

"…Ugh… Th-That was…"

"If it were me, young miss, I would be screaming and crying in fright."

"…I should probably apologize."

"Yes, I suppose so. But do take care, young miss. Perhaps he would start sobbing again at the very sight of you."

Anne's cool stare made my relief vanish. Now that I was thinking about it calmly, I supposed breaking down his door with an axe might have been a little overboard. *I was too freaked out by the Catastrophic Bad End… Why didn't I think of just picking the lock with a needle?*

Of course, I couldn't undo what was done. Hanging my head, I trudged back to Keith's room to apologize yet again. But when I got there, my brother welcomed me with a big smile on his face, saying, "You aren't to blame at all, Big Sister. I want to stay with you forever!" It was seriously the cutest thing.

In fact, Keith even begged for Mother to go easy on me. Thanks to that, I was allowed back at the dinner table that night. *My little brother is the absolute best — not only is he cute, but he also has such a gentle soul.*

And with this, the "Keith locked himself up inside his room?!" incident ended on a peaceful note, and I promised myself that I'd be sure to spoil him and make sure he'd never be alone again. The downside was that the situation made Mother decide that I needed lessons on social etiquette…

With that, I avoided yet another Catastrophic Bad End, but was forced to attend stuffy lessons on the manners of nobles by my demonic mother.

It was a spring day when my name became "Keith Claes." At the age of eight, this was already the second time I had my name changed.

The first time it happened was when I was three years old. Until then, I was told to keep quiet and sit in a tiny room. If I made any sound at all, I would be punished physically or have my meals taken away. I learned to obediently stay by myself, in a corner, silent and alone.

One day, a man I had never seen before took me away in a grand carriage before bringing me to a beautiful mansion. On that day, I met my father, along with my step-mother and half-brothers. Although I was still very young, I could tell from their cold stares that I was not welcome in the least.

From the rumors I had heard from the servants later on, it became clear to me that I was an unwanted child — my mother, who was a prostitute, had pushed me into the hands of my biological father. I was not allowed the privilege of calling my parents "Father" or "Mother," and I had to show deference when speaking to my brothers. In the beginning I didn't know how to speak formally, and so I was punished many, many times. I wasn't allowed a seat at the family dining table either; instead, I ate alone in my room.

My so-called parents largely ignored me and pretended I didn't exist, which didn't bother me much. My brothers, however, saw me as a target for bullying, and persistently stuck to this belief. They would punch me, kick me, and sometimes even lock me up in the storage shed for an entire day. And so I tried my best to avoid my half-brothers, and this was achieved by staying in my room for most of the day.

Then, one day, everything changed. I remember it well — the weather was fair, and I could see a small bird building a nest on a nearby tree. Engrossed in watching the bird go about its nest-building work, I forgot my place and slowly wandered out of the house to get a better view. Soon, I found myself standing by the tree.

Unfortunately for me, my brothers chose that moment to exit the house as well. They surrounded me and started to bully me. "You son of a whore!" they taunted as they kicked and punched me. I curled myself up as usual, enduring the pain as I waited for it to pass.

That was when it happened: one of my abusers noticed the small bird nesting in the tree.

"Hey. There's a bird there, see."

"Oh yeah, I see it. It has a lot of nerve building a nest on our land! Let's knock it down!"

My brothers started hurling rocks at the bird. Soon, the nest that the bird had worked so hard to build was destroyed in a shower of pebbles. And they didn't stop there; they threw rocks at the bird until it started making cries of pain.

"...Stop this!" I shouted without thinking. As the words left my mouth, something hot and searing seemed to pour forth from the depths of my heart and body.

Without warning, large objects fell from the sky. Before I knew it, my brothers were on the ground, their arms and legs pinned.

Scattered across the ground were some oddly-shaped pieces of packed dirt, approximately the size of an adult fist. They must have been the objects that had fallen from the sky. The bits of earth were quite hard, and they had left small craters where they had landed. My brothers had been hit and injured by some of these hard pieces of earth.

What happened? I could only stand there, shocked.

After a while, my brothers were carried to their rooms by some servants who had come out to check on them. A doctor was called.

From his diagnosis, it was discovered that my brothers suffered from multiple impact wounds across their bodies, and even had some broken bones.

I was the one who had injured them. Specifically, my Earth Magic had awakened, and I had used it against them.

From that day on, I became even more isolated and shunned. I was forbidden to leave my room unless absolutely necessary, and my brothers stayed away from me. In fact, they were completely terrified of me, and would run away screaming things like "monster!" And it wasn't just my brothers — even my parents and their servants avoided me. Though they didn't run away, I could see the fear in their eyes.

I couldn't stand the way they looked at me, so I kept myself cooped up in my room, staying as quiet as possible. Days, months, and eventually years passed. Then, another man I didn't know came to my room.

"In recognition of your high magical aptitude, it has been decided that you will be adopted into the Duke Claes household."

And just like that, I was packed into yet another carriage, to be brought to yet another place. Although I had lived in my father's house for five years, not a single person came out to say goodbye.

As soon as I arrived, I was struck by how much bigger and grander Claes Manor was in comparison to my previous home. From the intricate vases to the carpets and rugs lining the hallways, the place exuded an air of refinement. And my new father was none other than the master of the manor, Duke Claes.

"Hello, are you Keith? Welcome! Welcome to the Claes family," he said, addressing me with a smile. I had never been welcomed in such a way in my life — taken aback, I stood, perplexed and at a loss for words.

Almost immediately, the duke set about introducing me to the rest of his family. Madam Claes seemed somewhat aloof as she regarded me with a cold gaze. And then there was her daughter, the Duke's only child — Katarina Claes.

My half-brothers in the past bullied me on an almost daily basis, so honestly, the idea of having siblings terrified me. If possible, I wanted to give my new adoptive sister a wide berth, or at the very least just stay out of her way.

After a short exchange of introductions and pleasantries with Katarina, I was brought to my new room, and told to have some rest. Due to my sudden journey from my previous home, I was terribly tired, and soon fell asleep in the large, unfamiliar bed.

The very next morning, I sat at the breakfast table with the Claes family. This was the very first time I had eaten a meal with other people at the same table, and it was the best meal I ever had. My heart was filled with warmth.

After breakfast, I made to return to my room when Katarina unexpectedly approached me and offered to show me around the grounds. I had planned to steer clear of her, and was surprised when she approached me instead.

"I'll show you around the garden, Keith," she said.

Instinctively, I responded formally. "Thank you very much, Lady Katarina."

"Keith, we are brother and sister, you know. You should call me Big Sister! Also, you can drop the formalities with me," she said.

I was overcome with surprise. Up until now, I was not allowed to refer to any of my family members like that — not even my siblings. Yet, she still insisted.

"Ugh, we're siblings, Keith! It's fine! Also, I've always wanted a younger sibling to call me Big Sister! It's one of my many dreams!"

It would seem that Lady Katarina wished for me to address her as "Big Sister," and so I obliged. Katarina, seemingly greatly satisfied by this, responded with a happy smile.

With that, the two of us stepped out into the manor's grounds. Katarina, deciding to take advantage of the pleasant weather, led me around every corner of the gardens. After speaking with her for a while, I came to realize that Katarina Claes was a little... *different* than most noble little ladies.

"I'm pretty good at fishing. We should try it together next time!" she said, extending me an invitation. Before long she was off on another tirade, explaining passionately how she had tilled the earth and planted crops in some fields.

I had been cooped up in rooms all my life and had never fished or tilled the earth before, and I didn't remember seeing my half-brothers do anything of the sort. In fact, I was pretty sure that normal noble children would never do such things. All I could do was maintain a surprised expression as these thoughts raced through my head.

"I'll show you my favorite place next!" Katarina grabbed my hand and pulled me off in some direction.

Before long, we were standing before the tallest tree in the garden. "The view from up there is the best!" she said, her eyes sparkling with excitement. She then went on to tell me about how she was particularly skilled at tree-climbing.

When I told her that I had never done anything like it, she said "Well then! I will teach you all I know. First, watch my movements..."

Katarina kicked off her shoes and hiked up her dress. Before I could respond, she was off, climbing the tree enthusiastically.

I could only stand there, still shocked by what I was seeing. Katarina was making good progress, though the mortification of almost being able to see up her dress as she climbed took a toll on me. Katarina didn't seem to notice or care as she continued to quickly scale the tree's trunk.

Then, right as she was in the middle of her journey, she turned to me and waved with a big smile on her face. And then — Katarina lost her balance and swayed dangerously.

"Watch out!" I shouted as I ran up to the tree.

With a sudden thud, Katarina landed right on top of me. The impact of her fall passed through my body, and my consciousness seemed to fade.

After a while, however, I came back to reality, only to find myself in Katarina's arms.

"KEEEEITH! DON'T DIE!" Katarina wailed over and over again, until she finally realized that I was alright. "Keith?! Y... YOU'RE ALIVE!" she shouted, hugging me with incredible strength.

I froze up in shock. It was the first time I had been embraced by anyone.

"Wha— Does it hurt somewhere?" Katarina asked, concerned.

It was the first time anyone had ever worried about my well-being. Again, I was bewildered. It wasn't that I was seriously injured or felt any terrible pain. I was just unsure how to react to this situation.

But Katarina seemed to have mistaken my confusion for some sort of severe injury. "Wait here, Keith. I'll get some help and bring you back to the manor right away." She took off running, hiking up her dress and not even bothering to put her shoes back on. She raced towards the manor at an incredible speed. Watching her rapidly shrinking silhouette, I was filled with warmth, just like how I had felt at breakfast.

That very same night, Madam Claes called us all into her room and asked the duke for a divorce. After some conversation, it became evident that she had misunderstood several things, and the two were soon lovingly together again.

After that incident, Madam Claes' disposition seemed to change. She became gentle and kind towards me. Duke Claes himself was kind and loving too.

My adoptive sister, Katarina Claes, taught me many things. For example, I learned how to fish. "Keep this a secret from Mother, alright?" she said as she taught me how to climb trees. And when I was praised by our tutor for my skill at the sword, Katarina was as happy for me as if she herself were the one being praised.

Every day was vibrant and enjoyable. I felt truly blessed… and so I forgot. I forgot that I was a monster who had hurt others with my magic — dangerous magic that could not be controlled.

That day, Katarina and I visited the fields after our swordplay lesson. The various plants that Katarina had cultivated were finally starting to grow. As we spoke about the various aspects of fieldwork, the conversation shifted to the topic of magic.

"Yes! I'd like to try controlling an Earth Golem!"

An Earth Golem was made by infusing magic into a figure made of earth. It was an ability that I had, which I had discovered by coincidence some time ago. I had been playing with some dirt, shaping it into dolls while cooped up in my room. I didn't have any company, so I made these dolls and sat next to them as I had my meals.

However, I had promised Duke Claes that I would not use my magic. Although my magic was strong, I didn't have the skill to control it. Due to my history of injuring my half-brothers, the Duke was planning to find a magic tutor for me who would teach me how to control my abilities.

But Katarina was staring at me with such expectant eyes that I gave in and decided to show her just a little bit of my magic. She was greatly pleased with my little walking golem, and immediately asked if I could make it bigger. And so I did, only to find that I could not control a golem of that size.

Swept up in her excitement, Katarina approached the golem despite my warnings, and was soon sent flying by the golem's arm. Her small body soared through the sky. This time, I couldn't catch her — she fell head-first onto the cold, hard ground.

After she was transported to her chambers by some servants, a doctor was called to give Katarina an in-depth check-up. I was told that she had just hit her head and passed out, but otherwise she was fine.

I looked at Duke Claes, who was watching over his unconscious daughter with a concerned expression on his face.

"I broke my promise to not use magic, and I also hurt my big sister. It's all my fault, so I will accept any punishment. I am really, really sorry. Please feel free to chase me out of the household if you see fit…"

Duke Claes looked at me, visibly troubled. "About this incident… we should really wait to hear from Katarina after she has woken up. We will discuss it then. More importantly, Keith… You look really ill, as if you could fall over at any moment. Katarina will be fine for now. You should rest in your room."

With that, the Duke led me out of Katarina's room. That night, I heaved a sigh of relief as I heard that Katarina was going to be just fine. Although I wanted to go and meet her right away… I couldn't. I was afraid.

The very next morning, I couldn't bring myself to leave my room. For the very first time since I had lived in this manor, I missed breakfast. Then, around when breakfast time had ended...

"Keith! It's me, Katarina! You weren't at breakfast... Are you feeling okay?" Katarina's voice called to me from beyond the door.

"Big Sister..." Without thinking, I responded to her.

"Yes, it's me. What's wrong? Does your stomach hurt? Are you okay?" Although Katarina was the one who was injured by what I had done, she seemed more concerned about me.

"...Nothing is wrong... More importantly, how are your injuries, Big Sister?"

"I'm fine, it was just a little bump on the head! It doesn't matter. Keith... I'd like to speak to you. May I come in?"

I was relieved at how cheerful Katarina was. Honestly, I wanted to see her. I wanted to see her right away. But...

"I'm sorry. I cannot let you in."

"Wh... Why?"

"...I can no longer be by your side, Big Sister."

I wanted to see her. But no matter what I did, the image of Katarina passing out stayed anchored in my mind. I wanted to see that she was well and happy... But I couldn't do that. I could no longer be around Katarina.

I, being the monster I was with my magic that was perpetually out of control, would only be a danger to Katarina if I remained here. Gentle, kind Katarina, who taught me many, many things. I had hurt her.

Although Katarina continued talking at the door, I buried my head in the pillows, curling up into a ball on my bed. I was used to living alone in a small room, so I would continue living like this on my own. That way, I would never hurt anyone important to me ever again.

After a while, I could no longer hear Katarina's voice. I figured that she gave up on me, and I deserved it, after ignoring her for so long. That was all I could think about as I remained alone in the darkness.

"Keith, step back from the door."

I'd thought she had given up, but there was Katarina's voice again. I turned to look at the locked door, only to see it suddenly splinter and fall to pieces before my eyes.

Standing in the doorway and silhouetted by the light was Katarina, with a resolute expression and an axe in hand. Again, I was stunned. Katarina had destroyed the door to my room... and had now stepped into it.

"I'm sorry about yesterday!" Katarina was on her knees before my bed, and had lowered her head so deep that it touched the ground. "I'm really sorry for making you use your magic, and for being so pushy! And for not listening to your warnings about going near the golem! I'm so so sorry for worrying you!"

I slowly slid off of my bed and knelt next to Katarina. "...Why are you apologizing, Big Sister...? I am the one at fault..."

"What are you talking about?! I am the one who was wrong! I asked you to do something you didn't want to do, Keith!"

Why was Katarina approaching me? Why was she saying things like this? I was so sure she would be afraid of me, since I had hurt her with my magic.

"...Are you not... afraid of me, Big Sister?"

"Afraid?"

"...In my previous home, I ended up hurting my brothers with my magic. This time, I hurt you, Big Sister. Although my magic is strong, I can't control it at all... I always end up losing control and hurting people... Even so, are you not afraid of me, Big Sister?"

I told her of the incident that had happened before. With this, I was sure that Katarina would never want to see me again.

I was scared that I would hurt Katarina… but even more so, I was scared of the possibility that everyone would look at me like that again — with those eyes full of fear, like my previous family. I was afraid of being labeled a monster once more. This was why I refused to meet Katarina's gaze, even as she stormed straight into my room. If her eyes were filled with fear, I…

I held my breath, awaiting Katarina's next words.

"Ohh, that's what you meant!"

Those were not the words I was expecting. Confused, I slowly raised my head. My eyes met with Katarina's aqua-blue ones.

"If you can't control your magic, you just have to keep practicing, right? We'll have a magic tutor soon. We can practice together!" Katarina didn't have the slightest hint of fear in her eyes. Instead, she was smiling and her gaze was filled with a gentle warmth.

"…We can stay together, Big Sister?"

"Of course! I'll stay with you forever!"

Being alone was painful and sad. I wanted to be with someone. But no one wanted to be around me. If I approached them, they would shout at me, calling me "son of a whore" or "monster." I had all but given up and thought that no one would want to be with someone like me…. But there she was, a smiling young girl, saying that we'd be together forever.

"So, even if something bad happens again, you can't lock yourself in your room— Keith! What is it?! Are you hurt?!" Katarina raised her voice in alarm as she looked upon my face.

Wondering why she was so worked up, I raised a hand to my cheek… only to find that it was wet. Tears were streaming from my eyes. *Ah, I'm crying.* Like I did before, silencing my voice as best as

I could, cooped up in those tiny rooms. The tears would flow when things were hard, or when I was lonely. My chest would hurt, and I would only feel worse.

But then... what were these tears? The more I cried, the more my heart was filled with warmth. For the first time in my life, I discovered that people could cry when they were happy, too.

Katarina, apparently worried about me, started to pat me on the back. *Such gentle, warm hands.* That was all I could think as she continued to console me.

I want to stay by her side — by Katarina Claes' side. If possible... I would like to stay forever.

I resolved to master my magic, and be able to control it well — and then I would stay by Katarina's side and protect her with all my might.

The seasons passed, and soon it was summer. I, Katarina Claes, was now nine years old. For my birthday, I got a cute dress from Father and a bouquet of flowers from Keith. Mother gave me a mountain of books on manners and social etiquette.

Jeord came to me with a luxurious gift: a necklace with all sorts of expensive-looking gemstones on it. Of course, there was no way I could accept something like that, so I did my best to refuse it. The prince then asked what I wanted instead, and after some thought, I decided to ask for watermelon seedlings. It would be nice for my fields to have some fruit.

As usual, Jeord froze up and remained unmoving for a few moments after hearing my request for seedlings. But true to his word, he delivered quite a few impressive-looking plants the very next day. Not wanting to waste any time, I quickly had the seedlings planted. If the watermelons did bloom and bear fruit, I would be sure to share some with Jeord.

Father, who doted on me as usual, suggested holding a lavish birthday party for me. I didn't want that kind of attention, though, so I refused. Mother agreed with me on the grounds that I would make an embarrassment of myself, and convinced Father to listen to my request.

Unfortunately, we would have to hold a party when I turned fifteen. It was a kind of social debut, and was important to the family's reputation. Mother, who claimed that she would "do something about me by then," seemed a little too enthusiastic about the process. The thought of her already severe etiquette lessons getting even worse struck fear into my heart.

I had started training with my long-awaited magic tutor, who informed me that "communicating with one's origin" wasn't quite what I was imagining. I realized that tilling the earth and planting fruit wasn't going to increase my magical powers, but I continued my fieldwork as a hobby.

By the time we were a few months into our magic training, Keith had already developed a greater sense of control over his powers, as I knew he would. My Dirt Bump had improved from a two- or three-centimeter lump. It was now as tall as seven to eight centimeters! A great achievement indeed, at least for me. Perhaps I would soon be able to control Earth Golems, just like Keith.

While not exactly perfect, my life continued on peacefully, until…

"…Ahh. I wonder why…?" I said, kneeling down on the field.

I was flanked by Keith, my cute adopted brother, and Prince Jeord, who was now visiting Claes Manor every few days.

"What is it, Big Sister?"

"What is wrong, Katarina?"

Keith and Jeord both piped up, apparently curious.

I pointed at a corner of the field. "Look at that."

The plants in that specific corner were completely wilted. It would be harvest season soon, but that corner didn't look like it would yield anything worth picking.

"I've been taking care of the plants in that corner over there…"
I sighed again, feeling down. Why were the plants I cared for, and those alone, withering?

To tell the truth, I wasn't really good at taking care of plants in my previous life either. From morning glory flowers to cucumber plants, anything I touched would eventually shrivel up and die. But I had been reborn! Surely I would be able to raise plants perfectly this time… or so I thought. I gazed at my plants sadly.

"Big Sister, aren't you tired from your field work? Perhaps you should rest here for a while…"

"Indeed. It is best that you rest your body, Katarina."

Keith and Jeord spoke to me as I hung my head, both extending their hands, offering to help me up. Their eyes met.

"Prince Jeord, I will lead my sister to shelter. Also, it would be just fine if you did not show up for social visits so often."

"I am Katarina's future husband, Keith. I will escort her. In fact, it would be quite alright if you did not stick so close to her."

While the two never did meet in the game, both Keith and Jeord seemed to get along very well. They were both smiling, and seemed to have a lot of fun throwing jibes at each other. As the two cheerful boys talked next to me, I looked towards the corner and sighed yet again.

"Oh, Katarina. We have received an invitation to a tea party. Would you like to attend?" my father asked.

"Tea party?" I asked while stuffing my face full of bread. Mother shot me a murderous glance, and with a big gulp, I swallowed the bread as quickly as I could.

"Yes, a tea party. You are now nine, a good age for attending such a function, I would think."

It was apparently common in this world for nine- or ten-year-olds to attend tea parties, in preparation for their eventual social debut at age fifteen. The main aim, of course, was to let the children of nobles socialize with one another.

"I suppos—"

"Out of the question! My dear husband, Katarina is hardly armed with the prerequisite manners for such an affair!" Mother snapped, agitated by my response.

"Well... that may be true, but would she not learn a little through experience? Also, the invitation comes from a relative of mine, you see. They are not exactly strangers. I think it is a good opportunity for Katarina," Father said as he shot a sideways glance at me.

Hmm? What do you mean, "that may be true," Father? Why the sideways glance?

"...Yes, I suppose you are right. Perhaps she would learn the importance of it all, should she see it in person..." Mother said, turning to me. Her eyes were blank and hollow.

What's with the eyes, Mother?!

"Yes, Keith shall attend the party with her as well. We can all rest assured if Keith is with her," Father said, nodding his head in satisfaction. His expression seemed to suggest that he had come up with a breakthrough of a solution.

My mother readily agreed with him. "Yes, that's right. It'll be alright if Keith is with her." Come to think of it, my parents now thought very highly of my hard-working brother.

"Keith, would you go with Katarina to the tea party?"

"Yes father. I will be most pleased to go with Big Sister," Keith responded with a refined smile on his face.

Huh? But… But I'm the Big Sister here! Why am I being treated like a no-good problem child who has to be babysat by Keith?

And so, while there were a few things that didn't quite sit right with me about the situation, I ended up going with Keith to my very first tea party.

After even more lessons on manners and etiquette with Mother and an endless barrage of tips and warnings, the day of the tea party finally arrived. Father got me a newly-tailored dress to wear, and I accompanied Keith to the home of Marquess Hunt, the host of the party.

"Lady Katarina, Master Keith. Thank you very much for attending our family's tea party today."

The one who greeted us was Lillian Hunt, the eldest daughter of the Hunt family. She was a girl of fourteen with honey-colored hair and eyes, almost ready for her social debut. Standing behind her were three young girls who I assumed were her sisters. I thought I remembered that there were four daughters in the Hunt family.

Lillian's sisters introduced themselves in order of age — the second, then the third. Both of these two girls resembled their oldest sister. I returned their curtsies as best as I could, remembering what my mother had so desperately taught me.

After three of the four sisters had greeted us, a fourth girl with a shy and hesitant demeanor came forward. "…H-Hello… It is n-nice to meet you. I am the… fourth sister, M-Mary Hunt…" the girl introduced herself with an impossibly soft voice. Unlike her sisters, her hair and eyes were a deep shade of red, like a burnt sienna. She was beautiful in a different way, with big eyes and shapely lips.

Mary curtsied and I gave her one in return. But immediately after, she retreated behind her sisters and disappeared from view. ... *Is it because of my face? Because I look like some sort of villainess? I might look evil, but that doesn't mean I should be shunned!* I felt a tinge of sadness in my heart as the Hunt sisters excused themselves, apparently off to greet their other guests.

A few rules for this tea party had been drilled into my mind by Mother. For starters, I was to keep my mouth shut and shaped into an elegant smile as much as possible. Also, I wasn't supposed to stuff my mouth full of food or candies, or make slurping sounds when drinking my tea. Above all else, I absolutely must not hike up my dress and run around, even if I failed all the other rules. Mother stuffed so many rules into my head that I felt like it was going to explode.

This was why I tried harder on this day than any other to smile as elegantly as possible and to sip my tea in a ladylike way. After all, this tea party was practice for the great social debuts we all had to eventually attend.

The Hunt sisters, still making their rounds and issuing the appropriate greetings, didn't sit down for tea. Keith and I had to do the same thing, and before I knew it, we had circled the room several times. Only then did we stop for tea, which was good because I was getting tired.

Personally, I felt like I was really behaving myself, so surely a single cookie wouldn't hurt? I reached for the tray.

Oh? This cookie is super good.

Hmm. One more wouldn't hurt.

And another.

Oh ho? Do I spy a muffin on that tray?

I'll try one.

In fact, there seemed to be a lot of treats left on the trays. The other guests, seemingly lost in conversation, had hardly touched them. *What a waste! I should've brought along a little box to take home some with me. Maybe I could borrow one from the Hunts?*

"Big Sister."

"...K-Keith?!"

My brother had materialized out of nowhere and was standing behind me. Surprised at his sudden appearance, I jumped in response. We had gotten separated while making our rounds, but he had tracked me down.

"You surprised me, Keith! Are the introductions all over now?"

"Yes, they are mostly done. More importantly, Big Sister... why are you just standing here?"

"Umm..."

"You would not, perchance, be thinking of bringing back these leftover snacks in a small box, would you?"

"Ah?!"

Wow, Keith! Are you some kind of psychic? Uncanny!

"That's amazing, Keith! You know me so well!"

"...It is not a matter of me knowing you well. If you really went and did something like that, the reputation of the Claes family would be severely called into question... Also, Mother would definitely ban you from eating any treats for quite a while as punishment."

"...Ugh. You're right..."

In fact, Mother had reacted the same way when I picked up a fallen cookie from the ground and ate it during a recent etiquette lesson, citing the three-second rule. She didn't let me eat any kind of treat for three whole days. I could only imagine what would happen if I asked the Hunts for a box and came home with leftovers. A week-long ban, maybe?

That would be absolutely awful. Even though it was a bummer, I had to forget the idea of taking any treats home. But to make up for it, I stuffed my face full of whatever food I could get my hands on, completely forgetting about the promise I'd made to my mother.

Keith did try to warn me many times, but the exchange always went the same way: "Have you not had enough, Big Sister?" — "Oh, just a little more…" I would say as I continued gorging myself. After all, it would be a huge waste to leave all these snacks sitting around. They were so delicious!

Ah, so yummy! This one over here too, just one more…

Predictably, a familiar pain soon took over my stomach — a telltale sign that I had eaten way too many cookies, candies, and other treats. After reassuring a worried Keith that I was fine despite my distressed look, I took off running to search for the washroom.

When I found a servant of the house, I asked them for directions. They offered to guide me, but I had to turn them down and run off on my own instead. I'd never make it in time if I were elegantly guided by a servant.

To my relief, I did reach my destination in time. But I was in such a hurry getting there that I couldn't remember my way back to the reception area. Although the Marquess Hunt's manor was nowhere near as large as my father's, it was large enough to get lost in. It didn't take me long to realize that there was no way I'd be able to find my way back on my own.

I guess I could find another servant and ask. So I wandered the halls, only to stop dead in my tracks as I was met with an impossibly beautiful sight.

A sea of flowers stretched out before my eyes. It seemed to be some kind of indoor courtyard. Drawn in by the breathtaking scene, I found a door into the garden and went through it.

As soon as I set foot into the garden, a girl stood up, seemingly surprised at my entrance. Although I should have called out to her out of courtesy, I hesitated out of surprise. She was the first to speak.

"...L-Lady Katarina. Why are you in a place like this?" The girl was Mary Hunt, fourth daughter of the Hunt family, who I had met just a short while ago.

"...Um. For a ch-change of pace?" I couldn't tell poor Mary that I had stuffed my face with food, dashed to the backroom, and gotten lost on the way back. Anyway, there was nothing wrong with a little white lie — she didn't need to know the details.

"What are you doing here yourself, Lady Mary?" Even compared to having eaten too much and needing the washroom, I found it even stranger for one of the Hunt daughters to be hiding here on such an important occasion.

"...I am not very... good with crowds..." Mary replied, in that same soft, almost inaudible voice that she had greeted me with earlier.

She's such a beautiful girl! What a waste for her to be hiding herself away like this.

Hmm. Or maybe... is it really my face? Do I really look like a scary villainess?

Even if I did my best to smile, there was a high chance that this scary face of mine would scare the beautiful and fragile girl before me. I had to let her know that I was completely harmless!

"Th-This is quite the impressive garden. All these blooming flowers are stunningly beautiful, truly." I tried my best to dispel my villainess aura, delivering my lines with a smile on my face.

I really did feel that way about the garden, so the compliments were sincere. Although the Claes Manor gardens were respectable in their own right, this little garden had a unique charm of its own. The flowers in particular were so vibrant. The Hunt's gardener must be really good at their job.

That's right! What a great idea! If this mystery gardener was so skilled at growing flowers, maybe they could give me some gardening advice, and even help me revive my wilting crop corner.

With that in mind, I quickly asked Mary about it. "Say... Lady Mary, could you please introduce me to the gardener overseeing this magnificent garden?"

"...Huh...?"

"After all, these flowers are blooming splendidly! I would very much love to discuss certain matters with this amazing gardener of yours."

Despite Mary's increasingly uncomfortable expression, I inched closer steadily, my excitement causing my nostrils to flare as I heaped praise upon this mystery gardener.

Finally, Mary responded, in an almost inaudible voice. "...That... would be... me."

"Huh?"

"I... I am the one who takes care of this garden..."

What?! Mary is the caretaker of this wondrous garden?!

"All of it, Lady Mary?! You take care of this entire garden all by yourself?!"

"Well... Not all of it, just the plants in this little corner here..."

It turned out that Mary was responsible for the sea of blooming flowers in the corner that I had been staring at all this time.

"...Incredible."

"Huh...?"

"It's incredible, Lady Mary! You have cultivated such an impressive garden! What is your secret? How do you get the flowers to bloom like that? There must be some kind of trick. Is it the soil?!"

"...A-Ah... Um. Lady Katarina."

I was now dangerously close to Mary, having completely forgotten the concept of personal space. Before I knew it, I had cornered this poor, fragile young lady, and was breathing right in her face.

Not good. I had gotten far too excited. With a quick but deep breath, I took a small step back, assuming as elegant a smile as I could. "W-Well. I would very much like to discuss the particular details of how you have managed to cultivate such an impressive garden, Lady Mary."

"...Discuss? Particular... details?"

"Yes. Very much so." If possible, I wanted to discover Mary's secret before this summer's harvest season.

Although Mary seemed surprised at the fact that I had tilled the earth and seeded the fields myself, she listened carefully to my description of the problem. At least she didn't seem scared of me anymore, which was a huge relief. Eventually, I finished my explanation.

"...If someone like me could be of use, I would give it my all. However, Lady Katarina, I have never cultivated crops or vegetables before. I cannot make any assumptions on words alone... I deeply apologize for being unable to help."

"W-Well then! Could you come visit? Perhaps?" I said somewhat desperately to Mary, who was hanging her head.

"Ah, but..."

Although Mary seemed reluctant, I continued pleading, even suggesting that I arrive with a carriage and escort her to the manor. *The life of my crops is on the line! This is really important!* I thought, remembering the cruel fate of the morning glories and cucumber plants from my previous life.

95

Finally relenting under my continued assault, Mary agreed to pay a visit to Claes Manor and have a look at the crops herself. But she fervently refused to be picked up, apparently wanting to make the journey herself.

Now in a buoyant mood, I was safely led back to the reception area by Mary. Unfortunately, Keith then gave me an earful about being worried all this time at my sudden disappearance. For some reason, it felt like our big sister-younger brother relationship had been reversed.

And so the first tea party in my life came to a pretty uneventful end, rather than the huge social disaster it could have been.

A few days after the tea party, Mary paid a visit to Claes Manor, as promised. To address the problem my crops were facing, Mary even read up on crop cultivation in advance. *She's so kind and thoughtful!*

I found out that we were the same age, and after some conversation, we became fast friends. Although she was somewhat afraid of me at first, Mary was now all smiles. And my crop corner seemed like it would eventually recover, though it would take countless visits from Mary.

"Mary... thank you so much! Because of you, the crops are doing well again!" I said cheerfully, gazing at the restored crops.

"No, you worked hard too, Lady Katarina," Mary replied with that same gentle smile on her face.

Being smiled at by such a lovely girl is a sight for sore eyes!

"I was sure they would all wilt and die... But now look! You're really something else, Mary."

"...Th-That's not true..."

Despite her humble demeanor, Mary really had a talent at cultivating plants. It seemed like her very hands breathed life into ailing plants of all kinds. *Yes, Mary's hands are special. Come to think of it, isn't there a term for this sort of thing?*

"You have a green thumb, Mary! Maybe even green hands too, ha!"

"...Green thumb?"

"Yes, a green thumb. It means you have a particular talent for cultivating plants. Of course, it's more than just your thumb... Special hands, maybe!"

"...Special hands..."

"Yes! With your talented hands, you breathe life into dying plants! You're amazing at it!"

I held Mary's hands firmly in my own. Mary had her eyes wide open, and was preoccupied with staring at her hands, now clasped in mine.

"...My hands are special...?"

"Yes! You have a real talent. You're a special and wonderful person!" I said, laughing. Mary smiled ever so slightly in response. Her smile was like a blooming flower.

"Lady Katarina, your fields have now recovered, but... would it be possible, perhaps, for me to visit you again?"

"Of course! Come visit anytime!" I declared, laughing wholeheartedly. Although Mary was so reserved when she asked me, she seemed pleased by my response as I saw her off.

"A green thumb is really quite remarkable, isn't it?" said Keith, who had been standing quietly next to me this whole time.

"Yes! Especially if they are on hands like Mary's! She works wonders on plants."

97

"Yes. A long time ago, I read a book called *The Girl with the Green Thumb,* so I've heard the phrase. Did you read that book too, Big Sister?

"Hmm... I don't think so, Keith. At least, it wasn't from a book... Somehow it just popped into my head." *I remembered the term when I looked at Mary. Where did I learn it from?*

"That aside, Big Sister. Lady Mary has sure become more cheerful lately."

"That's right! Although... she was quite afraid of me at first."

"Hm? Afraid of you, Big Sister?"

"...Yes, unfortunately. It has to be this villainess-looking face of mine," I replied, feeling sorry for myself. *I really hate this evil-looking face that I got from my mother.*

Keith seemed surprised. "...I don't really think you look like a villainess, Big Sister... Also, Lady Mary did not act that way towards you alone — she was like that with everyone at the party."

"...Huh? Really?"

"Yes. She is very shy regardless of who she is speaking with. Perhaps there are certain circumstances in the family that have made her lose her confidence."

"...Circumstances? What do you mean?" I asked, puzzled.

Keith could only stare back with a look of exasperation. "What exactly were you doing at the Hunt manor, Big Sister? Were you not listening to the conversations at the tea party at all?"

"...Ugh..." Come to think of it, as soon as we finished our greetings, I was too busy thinking about taking leftover food back home. And after Keith caught me, I immediately started stuffing my face.

In the end, I hardly talked to anyone at the tea party. *But hey, that's why my lack of noble etiquette stayed a secret! Yep, that was my plan all along. Let's leave it at that.*

As if giving up on me, Keith sighed deeply. *Sorry, my dear brother.*

Keith slowly explained what he had heard at the tea party to his hapless sister. From what he said, it would seem that out of the four Hunt sisters, only Mary looked different. The reason for this was that Mary, the fourth sister, had a different mother.

Marquess Hunt's first wife had died of illness, and after he remarried, he had a child with this new wife. That was Mary. But since Mary's mother was of lower social status, the marriage wasn't welcomed by either of their families. To make things worse, Mary's mother became sick and passed away when she was only five years old. While the Marquess did what he could to care for Mary, her sisters had no love for her. They would torment her every day, claiming that the "stench of commoners oozed from her being," or that she "had no class."

"So that was why Mary acted like that..." I couldn't blame her. It was no surprise that someone who was treated like that every day would lose confidence in themselves. She must have thought something was wrong with her, which would make her afraid of talking to others.

"However, she has changed very much since then. I believe Lady Mary will be alright," Keith said with a compassionate expression.

Does my hardworking brother know something else about the situation? I tried asking him about it, but he deflected the question.

While Keith himself had been reserved and fearful when he'd first come to the manor, he had changed a lot during these past few months. He tried really hard at his etiquette and magic lessons, and had proved himself to be a mature and dependable kid.

Although I told him he didn't have to grow up so fast, Keith said that he was doing it so he could protect what was important to him. He even sounded mature as he told me that, and it made me feel lonely. Any time I tried to find out what he was trying to protect, he dodged the question and I could only sulk in response.

"By the way, is Lady Mary not soon to be engaged to Prince Alan?"

"...Oh? Yeah probably," I responded, halfheartedly agreeing with Keith. While I would have liked for him to stay my cute little brother for a little while longer, it seemed like Keith was quickly maturing into a young adult.

And again... what's this thing he wants to protect? What if... Wait. Is there a girl he likes?! Hold on, wait up! You should at least introduce this mystery girl to your Big Sister! I won't allow any strange girls into this... Hmm? Keith seems to be saying something.

"...Keith. Could you please repeat yourself?"

"...Big Sister..." Keith stared at me, exasperation plastered across his face once more.

Ah, sorry again, brother.

"As I was saying, it will soon be time to announce Lady Mary's betrothal to Prince Alan."

"...Hm? Who's Mary getting engaged to again?"

"Prince Alan. Don't you remember? Prince Jeord's twin brother, the fourth-born prince?"

"Huh?!"

"As she is now, there is a high chance that Lady Mary will be announced as Prince Alan's future bride."

"...She's engaged to Prince Alan?"

"Well... it has not been confirmed yet, but now would be a good time for it. The Hunt family is known for its riches and high social position, even amongst the other marquesses. She is a fitting candidate for the prince, as they are of the same age as well... Big Sister, where are you going?!"

After listening to a little over half of Keith's explanation, I ran off, heading straight for my room. *Prince Alan... Alan Stuart. He's one of the possible love interests in the game!*

Rushing back to my room, I quickly retrieved the "*Fortune Lover* Unofficial Strategy Guide" to cross-check its contents. After laying out the guide on my desk, I flipped through its pages rapidly before eventually coming to a stop at Prince Alan's page.

Alan Stuart.

Jeord's twin brother, the fourth-born son of the King. Up until the age of five, he was so sickly that his caretakers were scared that he wouldn't live long. Because of this, everyone around him did everything they could to ensure that they would survive, and ended up spoiling him in the process.

Due to this, his personality is a little twisted — although nowhere near Jeord's level. Feeling a massive inferiority complex due to Jeord's savant-like capabilities, he hardly spoke to his older brother, seeing him as an arch-rival.

At the age of fifteen, Alan would enroll in the academy with his brother, and often compete with him both academically and magically. Yet when the results of the academy's first test are published, Alan comes in third, with Jeord in first place and the protagonist in second.

While Alan had resigned himself to the fact that he could never outdo his brother, he takes great offense to being bested by a commoner girl, and in turn views her as a rival too.

After some interaction, Alan would eventually fall for the protagonist, charmed by her optimistic nature. As the game progresses, the protagonist would tell him "You are perfect as you are, Alan." This declaration brings some peace to his heart, and eventually Alan's bitter sense of rivalry with Jeord would diminish as well.

In this scenario, Katarina Claes, all-time villainess, was nowhere to be seen. Although she did attempt to bully the protagonist due to her good grades (despite being a commoner), she did not have much screen time in this route at all.

In Katarina's place was another rival: none other than Mary Hunt, daughter of Marquess Hunt. Although she respects Alan from the bottom of her heart and is somewhat jealous of the protagonist, she doesn't engage in any bullying or mean tricks.

Instead, Mary conducts herself as a noble lady with excellent upbringing, being skilled at social etiquette and dancing, unlike the commoner-born protagonist. Although Jeord hardly cares about Katarina's existence in the game, Alan is quite fond of Mary, although not in a romantic sense. Instead, he sees her like a little sister, and the two get along well.

In fact, even the endings of the game were different. If the protagonist gets the happy end and succeeds in romancing Alan, Mary gives them her blessing, asking the protagonist to "take care of Prince Alan from here on out." But her eyes would be filled with tears throughout the moving scene.

In the bad ending scenario, Mary and Alan live happily ever after instead, and that was that.

I thought intensely about the information I had just processed.

How come only Katarina ends up suffering?! Isn't Mary a rival character too? You don't see her desperately escaping Catastrophic Bad Ends!

Anyway, why is Mary such a gracious character even though she's a rival?! Katarina is the only one who's a villainess, apparently?

What were the staff behind this game thinking?! Why do they only subject Katarina and no one else to these terrible scenarios?! That character design is just too depressing! You people should try being reborn as Katarina Claes just once, let's see how you like that!

And then there's Alan! Why does he get a nice ending either way? Look at Jeord, or Keith! They end up becoming murderers and disappear into the wild! This is completely unreasonable! I'll never forgive you, Fortune Lover *staff!!*

If I ever find my way back to my old world, I'm totally going to storm into their offices and tear them a new one!

...I guess I should set aside my one-woman tirade for now. I turned to the page once again. There was no mistaking it; "Mary Hunt" was my lovable friend. But the Mary in the game was the perfect image of a noble lady. This didn't match the shy Mary that I currently knew.

Come to think of it, Mary and Katarina weren't exactly friends in the original setting. If anything, Mary didn't like Katarina very much because of the way she'd always use the Claes' social standing to do anything she wanted.

So Mary was a rival character like me all along... Even so, I didn't remember Mary ever mentioning Alan. I could only assume that they hadn't met, since their engagement hadn't been announced yet.

103

From what I could recall from the game, Mary told the protagonist about how she had met Prince Alan. It went like this:

From a young age, Mary had been bullied due to the fact that she was born of a different mother than the rest of her sisters. Her older sisters would verbally abuse her at every opportunity. This would eventually lead to Mary losing all of her confidence, believing that she was as useless as her sisters said she was.

Prince Alan was the one who appeared before Mary in her despair, praising the plants that she had raised in her garden. "You're amazing, Mary. You've really got a green thumb." It was a manner of speech that meant that she had a particular talent at raising plants. Alan, impressed by Mary's garden, praised her and told her that she was a special person.

This caused Mary to regain her lost confidence over time, and before she knew it, she was hopelessly in love with the prince. Mary worked hard daily to become a woman that could one day stand at the prince's side, and received nothing but praise during her time at the academy.

Katarina, on the other hand, spent all her time chasing after Prince Jeord, and so she lagged behind terribly on her academic and magic studies. She was nothing compared to Mary.

Mary really is a special person. Amazing Mary with the green thumb! Prince Alan sure has a way with words.

…Green thumb… Wait a minute! So this was where I heard the phrase before!

Ah, yes. I finally remember. Right, right. It was the memorable line that Prince Alan said to Mary… that she had a green thumb, that her hands were special, and all that.

...Hmm? Why do I remember saying something similar to Mary? Uh-oh. This is bad! Did I end up using Alan's line before he had a chance to say it?!

How could this be? What was I thinking? I can't just go around spouting memorable lines like that before the rightful user says them!

What should I do?! Now Prince Alan's line would be a rehash with as much impact as an already-brewed bag of tea leaves! A line like that only has half as much meaning the second time it is used!

Ahh, Katarina Claes, you absolute fool! If only I'd realized this sooner...

Although I spent some time lamenting in my room, I eventually cheered up when I realized that I couldn't change what was said and done.

After all, Prince Alan is a pretty good prince in his own right! I'm sure he'll be fine; it was just a single line. In fact, I'm sure he'll come up with an even better line, one that will steal Mary's heart! Yes, there's nothing wrong with me taking one of his lines! Nothing at all.

Having reached this irrefutable conclusion, I was overcome with relief. I packed up the guide and headed out of my room, making my way back to Keith, who I had so rudely abandoned a short while ago.

Mary Hunt is my name. I was born as the fourth daughter of Marquess Hunt's family. Although my mother was a beautiful and gentle person, she was not accepted in the Hunt family due to her low social standing. I, her daughter, was treated the same way.

Even so, Father and Mother loved me very, very much. With her unfortunate death, however, my life was greatly changed. With Father being away from the manor most of the time for work and my mother now gone, I felt like I did not belong anywhere in this manor.

While they were cold and distant to me when Mother still drew breath, now that she was gone, my older sisters wasted no time before viciously bullying me. They would hide my things, and sometimes even break them... or say terribly unpleasant things about me.

They would say things like: "Look at that red hair of yours! How filthy!", "The stench of commoners oozes from your being!", "You have absolutely no class!", "Know your place!", "You are nothing but a bringer of misfortune!", and so on.

Assaulted with all these words day by day, I felt my heart crumble, and slowly started to become frightened of interacting with others. This sense of fear permeated my being. Eventually, I started to believe what my sisters said — that I was no good, and that I would never amount to anything.

My only escape was the small garden in the courtyard. My heart only felt at ease while caring for the plants there.

One day, however, I met her — during a tea party that the Hunt family had organized. Although I was fearful and timid, she spoke openly and cheerfully to me. Her name was Katarina Claes. She responded to my fearful greeting with a bright one of her own. It was as if she were a being from another world.

Unable to get over my fear of people, I had left the tea party halfway through, having reached my mental limit. I quickly escaped to the small garden... but there, amidst the blooming flowers, was Katarina Claes. After gallantly venturing into the garden, Katarina had nothing but praise for what she saw. She complimented the garden I had been taking care of all this time.

I had not been praised in this manner by anyone — not since mother's death. Caught unawares, I withdrew into myself once more. It was then that Katarina suddenly asked for a favor. She wanted me to have a look at the fields she tended to, on account of their ill condition.

Honestly speaking, I was surprised at hearing that the oldest daughter of a duke would tend to fields of any kind at all. But I couldn't help but adore Katarina's sparkling eyes and plainly visible passion.

One thing led to another, and soon I found myself headed to the Claes family manor to help Katarina with her fields. I dedicated myself to learning about crops as much as I could so that I would be better able to assist her.

Unlike me, Katarina was bold and optimistic. She was a most admirable person. With Katarina's praise, I soon started regaining what confidence I had lost.

"You have a green thumb, Mary! Maybe even green hands too, ha! Yes! You have a real talent. You're a special and wonderful person!"

I had thought that I was nothing more than a weakling, a no-good girl who could never accomplish anything. However... Katarina said that I was a special, wonderful person.

I was so, so happy. I felt that now, more than ever, I had to become someone who was fit to stand next to Katarina. I had to be a worthy friend.

And so... I would bid farewell to the cowardly, weak Mary Hunt. One day, surely, I would be able to stand next to her proudly. Yes — I would work hard to become such a person.

A few weeks after the fields had been so magnificently resurrected, we entered the height of summer. It was then that the news of Mary and Prince Alan's formal engagement reached Claes Manor.

Since I invited Mary to come to the manor today, I promptly decided to ask her about it myself. "I heard about your engagement announcement, Mary. Congratulations!"

"Yes, thank you very much. I have been formally engaged to a prince, just like you, Lady Katarina. I am very much pleased."

While Mary did seem somewhat happy, I couldn't help but notice that she wasn't as thrilled as I would have expected.

"Umm. Have you met with the prince yet, Mary?"

"Yes, I have indeed met him."

"...Well? How was it?"

"How was... what, Lady Katarina?"

"Uh... well, you know. What was he like? And all that."

To be fair, I was guilty of unintentionally stealing one of the prince's memorable lines. Would Alan be able to charm Mary without that line?

"He is a most handsome person. He praised my garden as well, Lady Katarina — much like how you had done."

"O-Oh. And then...?"

Yes, this was all correct, scenario-wise. But the second half of Mary's response caught my attention.

"And then? What do you mean, Lady Katarina?"

"Umm. What happened after he showered praise on your garden?"

"Well, that was all there was to it...?" Mary replied, tilting her head slightly in apparent confusion.

WHAT?! That's all there was to it? Well, well what about that memorable line?! Didn't he say it?

"Um. Ahem. Did he say anything about your green hands— um, thumb?"

"...Green thumb, ah! Have you heard about what happened, Lady Katarina?"

"...I mean, he did say something like that, right? He did! Right?!"

As I continued questioning her, Mary, who was now positively blushing, offered up a token resistance before eventually giving in.

"My, how embarrassing... To think that you would hear of the affair yourself, Lady Katarina..."

"Hmm. Yes, as I expected, he did say tha— wait. What do you mean by 'affair'...?"

"Ah. Well, it is as you may have heard, Lady Katarina. I told Prince Alan about how you had praised me, saying that I had a green thumb..."

"WHA?! You said it to him?! And you told him I said it to you?!"

"Yes... Well. I was really happy that you would praise me in such a way, Lady Katarina... So happy was I that I had to tell Prince Alan about it too..." Mary said, her voice becoming gradually softer as the crimson hue on her face deepened.

So... how should I summarize this?

Before Alan could even claim that Mary was a special girl with a green thumb, I said it to her? Not only that, Mary went on to tell Alan that... "Ah, Lady Katarina mentioned that I had special hands... a green thumb..."

Faced with such a spectacle, there was no way Alan could say his line. After all, I said it first... or at least, something way too similar.

Oh no, Alan... I am sorry.

After my continued interrogation, Mary claimed that she liked the prince — but it was plain to see that she didn't *like* like him.

I am so, so sorry, Alan!

Well... they're engaged to each other anyway, so... I'm sure she'll learn all about the prince's charms from here on out!

...Work hard, Alan, I thought, my eyes glazing over as I continued my internal monologue. Mary, apparently worried about my faraway gaze, asked if I was hungry. *You really are the very image of a noble lady, Mary.*

Although it was by accident, I had somehow gotten between the two of them! This was no good. They should live happily ever after!

As much as I hoped it were possible, I didn't think I had the capability to bring the two together. All I could do was cheer for them from the depths of my heart.

A few weeks after my conversation with Mary, harvest season was nearing its end. It was a good time for the vegetables to be harvested and eaten.

"Young miss! The Prince is here, saying that he requires your presence!" Anne said in a tone of panic.

"What's the problem, Anne? Prince Jeord always marches in here whenever he wants either way."

While I used to make an effort to formally greet Prince Jeord when he came to visit, he told me not to after he started visiting more often. These days he showed up every three days or so, and would usually just walk into the garden where I was working in my overalls. He was used to seeing me in my gardening gear, so there was no reason for me to change into fancy clothes. Basically, the Prince visiting me was nothing out of the ordinary, and there was no reason for panic.

"No, you misunderstand, young miss! Your visitor is not Prince Jeord!"

"...Hmm?" *What's she going on about? Unless there's a social party or something, the only prince that comes here is Jeord*, I thought, giving one of my cucumbers a good pull.

"It isn't Prince Jeord, young miss! It's Prince Alan, the fourth prince of the kingdom!"

"...Huh?" I responded, stunned. The cucumber that I had held moments ago slid out of my gloved hands, falling onto the ground. "...Why?"

"I do not know the reason. In any case, you really should meet with him."

For some reason, I feel like this is the start of another mess...

After dashing back into the manor at full speed, Anne promptly helped me get dressed and then I headed off to the guest parlor. I hurried all the way to the doors and threw them open to find a haughty-looking boy standing with his back to me.

"You took your sweet time," the Prince said, turning his head to glance at me without introducing himself.

What a prick! Before I knew it, my cheeks started puffing out. *First he marches into my house, and now this?* I was close to losing my temper. But I reminded myself that he was an eight-year-old boy, whereas I was an adult of seventeen plus nine years of age, and instead offered a formal greeting.

"I offer my sincere apologies. I was caught up in some other affairs. I am Katarina Claes."

"Alan Stuart," the Prince responded haughtily in the face of my smile and formal manner of speech.

Alan Stuart... A potential love interest in Fortune Lover. *Wow, he's so pretty.* He didn't look at all like Jeord, who looked like a fairy-tale prince with his blonde hair and blue eyes. Alan had the same color eyes but had silver hair, giving him a wild and dashing image.

But even so, he was super arrogant, even for a prince. In fact, his attitude reminded me of Katarina Claes — at least, how I was before I regained all my memories. Even Jeord, who was a prince himself, would never behave like this. While he was twisted in his own way and definitely had some dubious ways of thinking, at least he was humble on the surface. I watched him and waited for him to speak as I wondered what his problem was.

"Katarina Claes. I am here because I have something to say to you today," the stuck-up Prince said, turning his steely gaze towards me.

"...Um. What is it?" As far as I knew, I had nothing to do with Alan. Well, I was engaged to Prince Jeord, so I guess that was something. But from what I remembered about *Fortune Lover*'s story, Alan avoided his brother as much as possible. So he shouldn't have had any special reason to visit me.

"You know Mary Hunt, right?"

"Huh...? Ah, yes." *Hm? What about Mary?*

"Mary said that you are close to her."

"...Yes? I suppose we are close friends."

Alan's gaze sharpened. *What the heck is his problem? What's he trying to say?*

"Did you know that Mary Hunt is now my fiancée?"

"Well, yes... I do know that."

"So you do know. Stop seducing her, then!"

"…S-Seduce?! What?!"

I could feel Alan's gaze digging into me and I swallowed in spite of myself. *Wait wait wait. What is he even saying? Is he out of his mind?*

Me, seduce Mary…? But we're both girls, for starters! Well yes, Mary is gentle, cute, and I like her a lot. I hope we can be friends for a long time. But I've never thought of taking her as my bride! I… I don't swing that way!

I want to get along with her from here on out… but at no point in time have I thought of taking Mary as my bride! I don't swing that way!

Alan clenched his teeth at my stunned silence. "Don't play dumb! Every time I ask her out, she says no! She's all like 'Oh, today I have an appointment with Lady Katarina.' In fact, *you* are all she talks about when she's with me! Mary has a pure heart, so clearly you're at fault for seducing her! There's no other explanation!"

"Wh-What is that supposed to mean?! I'm not going to stand here and listen to this nonsense!" It seemed like Alan wanted to pick a fight with me from the start. He got me all riled up and I started shouting, forgetting about being polite.

"What nonsense? This is the truth! With that face of yours, you've corrupted my pure Mary!"

So this stuck-up prince has decided that I'm a villain just because of my face. Well if there's one thing he's good at, it's pissing people off!

"What is wrong with you?! I've done no such thing! In fact, it's YOUR fault for asking Mary out when she already has plans to visit me! If you were really charming, no girl would turn down your invitation! You're CHARM-LESS! Mary keeps talking about me?! Well of course she would! It's because you're BORING!" I shouted, filled with a righteous rage. But I soon regretted my outburst.

113

"…Charm-less… Boring…" Alan's expression became stony.

…This is bad. I've finally gone and done it… I've said something terrible to a prince. And this had all started because I accidentally used his line. And I couldn't take that back now. I felt beads of cold sweat trickle down my back.

"…Ha. Haha. This is the first time I've been ridiculed to my face…" Steam seemed to be coming out of Alan's ears. He was positively livid.

"…Um. That just now was…" *Oh nooo, this is what I get for losing my temper! Now I can't take back what I said!*

"Prepare yourself, Katarina Claes. I shall take your train of insults as a thrown gauntlet."

Wait, wait. I haven't thrown any gauntlets! I'm not going to challenge anyone to any duels! It was just a slip of the tongue…

"I challenge you to a duel!" Alan said, his chin held high.

"…So. How did this happen, again…?" Anne said, with something between confusion and exasperation on her face.

We were now standing in the gardens of Claes Manor. To be specific, we were standing before two tall trees, conveniently located side by side.

"Well, Prince Alan did proudly proclaim 'I shall let you, the woman, decide on the contents of the challenge'… and so I did."

"…Even so! You are the daughter of a duke, young miss! And he is one of the princes of the kingdom! The two of you… climbing trees? This is going too far…"

"Well, I couldn't think of anything else I would do better in, so…"

"B-But young miss! Prince Alan does not climb trees! Did you not see how he froze when he heard your suggestion?"

"…But he was the one who accepted the terms, you know…"

Just like Anne said, Alan had frozen up as soon as I said the words "tree-climbing." In fact, he just stood there, staring at me for a while. Feeling concerned, I'd asked him *"Are you unable to climb trees, Prince Alan?"* He responded curtly, saying *"Of course not! I accept your challenge!"* and snapping out of his frozen pose.

This was how both Prince Alan and I had ended up standing in front of a pair of tall trees in the gardens of Claes Manor. My wise and gentle brother, Keith, was keeping Mother busy so she wouldn't notice the spectacle.

The rules of the challenge were simple: the first to reach the top wins.

Although Alan stood and gaped at the tree for a while, he eventually rolled up his sleeves as if steeling his resolve. It was only the Prince's entourage who were panicking. The servants pleaded things like, "Oh, my prince, it is most dangerous!" and "Please, please stop this at once!"

Meanwhile I had changed into an outfit with pants — I was fully prepared. "Well then, Prince Alan. Are you ready?"

"…Yeah. Right. Anytime."

"We'll begin on the count of three. Anne, my personal maid, will do the honors."

"Y-Yeah."

I had dragged the reluctant Anne into my challenge. With her count, the bout began — and then promptly ended with my overwhelming victory.

I climbed trees all the time, so I reached the top in minutes. Alan, on the other hand… *Umm, has Alan ever climbed a tree in his life?* When I got to the top of the tree, he was still stuck on the lowest branch. Before I knew it, the challenge had been completed.

"We have a clear winner. Can we all move on now?" I called down to him. *Hmph. Don't think you can defeat me, the wild monkey of the back hills, little boy. Have you even touched a tree before?*

While I turned to Alan with a victorious smile, he stared at me with a determined look in his eyes, clearly unwilling to accept defeat. "Again! I challenge you again! This is the first time I've climbed a tree — I just wasn't used to it!"

Whoop, there it is. So the Prince himself admits that he's never climbed a tree before. Maybe you should have said so from the very beginning, you show-off.

"No problem. But don't think you can win so easily, Prince."

"Bring it on!"

Alan challenged me again and again that day, but the result never changed, obviously. Eventually...

"I'll win next time! Just you watch!" Alan said, spouting the typical lines of a defeated rival character. After threatening to show up for another challenge sometime in the future, the Prince and his entourage left the grounds.

While I didn't know it then, I would continue humoring Alan's challenges for a long time after that. He showed up again a few days later, shouting about a rematch. Of course, I defeated him easily. But then he just kept showing up, wanting to try again. He would be defeated, then come back, and for a while this pointless pattern repeated itself.

As the days passed, we ended up striking up an odd friendship of our own. Alan and I developed a routine where we would have tea after each challenge. Maybe I was imagining it, but the Prince seemed happier lately despite his long string of losses.

Alan's change in attitude made me think that the conflict between me and the Prince was over, but then, one day...

"Jeord?! What are you doing here?!"

It was only a matter of time before Alan and Jeord ran into each other at the manor. Jeord visited every few days, while Alan visited once a week. Statistically, they were bound to come face to face. Mary, who visited twice a week, had already ended up meeting and introducing herself to Jeord.

Although I'd mentioned to Jeord that Alan and I had been having contests, I didn't mention to Alan that Jeord was around so often. My engagement to Jeord was public knowledge, but since Alan got so moody whenever the topic of his brother came up, I didn't want to tell him about his visits.

And so the two twin brothers, who hardly ever spoke to one another, met on the Claes Manor grounds.

"You sound as if me being here is a most mysterious thing. This is the home of my fiancée — my presence here is to be expected," Jeord said, regarding his twin brother with a smile.

I mean, he's right about that. But even so, Jeord does come around a lot. Is this just how everyone is in this world?

"...Doesn't matter. I'm here for a challenge with her today. Don't get in the way." For some reason, Alan seemed to have lost his edge. What happened to his unbearably haughty attitude? And while Alan was acting strange, so was Jeord. His ever-present smile was a lot more suspicious. It even looked a little malicious.

"About those challenges... I heard that you have failed to achieve victory, time and time again. Would it not be best to simply give up...?"

While I sometimes thought the same thing, I never would have said it to Alan so bluntly. I looked between them fearfully, afraid that Alan might snap and start raging. But his expression wasn't angry — he looked like he was in pain.

"…No! NO! We still need to settle it! I can win this! I… I know I can…!" Alan shouted desperately. He seemed to be focused entirely on his brother.

The tension in the room was so thick you could cut it with a knife. *This is bad… I guess I have no say in a fight between two brothers, but still, I have to do something.*

Alright then, clearly the solution is to change the subject. I had to clear away the miasma that was hanging in the air. And I had just the thing, something that had been on my mind for a while now.

"…Um, Prince Alan. If you don't mind, maybe we could change the terms of the challenge? If we keep climbing trees my mother will eventually find out, and she'll be really mad."

Honestly, it was kind of a miracle that Mother hadn't noticed up until now, and I didn't want to push my luck any further. She had given up on me a while ago — if I wanted to climb trees, then so be it — but inviting a prince to do the same… Well, she'd be enraged to say the least. Keith kept her occupied during Alan's visits, but she would eventually become suspicious about what I was up to. If I didn't change the challenge, I might get myself in big trouble… again.

"…If you say so… What will the new challenge be?"

"…Hmm."

Finally, Alan had turned to look at me and the disturbing atmosphere had started to fade. *Whew, good.*

Even though I was the one who came up with the idea, I wasn't sure what to replace tree-climbing with. My magic and academic abilities were average at best, and so I didn't want to choose anything like that. There was the option of intentionally letting him win, which might finally satisfy him. But that just wouldn't feel right.

As I continued scratching my head and trying to come up with a replacement, someone from Alan's entourage humbly presented a potential solution. "Pardon me, Lady Claes, but would a board game not be safe? No one would be hurt that way."

Alan's servant was right — board games are safe and appropriate for both genders. But I was notoriously bad at them. Whether it be chess or Othello, if it involved thinking, I was bad at it. In this world, chess was apparently the most popular board game, but naturally I wasn't a fan of it. While I knew how to play, I was always a sore loser when I was defeated.

Seeing my frown, Alan's servant provided a different option. "Ah. Well then, how about a musical contest? A contest of instruments, perhaps? The better performer would win, yes?"

That could be a refreshing change. In this world, being able to play an instrument was an important skill for the nobility, so I had learned the piano and violin from a young age. And in my previous life, I had been in student concerts playing the recorder and piano. I could still play the piano pretty well, but the violin and I were not suited to each other.

"I don't mind playing the piano," I responded cheerfully, and Alan agreed.

With this, the challenge between Alan and me was switched from a tree-climbing race to a musical competition. Somehow things had gotten really aristocratic when I wasn't looking. Well, at least Mother wouldn't be upset if she caught us competing.

The servants were united in relief, with most of the prince's entourage saying things like "Ah, what a relief that all this tree-climbing business is over and done with..." In fact, the servant who had suggested the musical idea was fervently praised by their peers.

And so, all of us headed for the music room, for the purpose of this safe and dignified musical bout. Claes Manor, naturally, had a huge piano that was much larger than the one I used to play back in school. The judges of the competition would be the servants of both our families and Jeord. I would be first to play, followed by Alan.

I sat down on the bench and turned towards the piano. I could only play "Der Flohwalzer" in my previous life, but as Katarina I had practiced from a young age. We were using a score sheet of a practice song aimed at beginners and young children.

Although I made some minor mistakes here and there, I felt like I played pretty well. In fact, Jeord seemed surprised — though that was probably more at the fact that I could play piano at all. ... *Should I take that as a compliment?*

Next up was Alan, who turned to the piano and promptly started playing. For the sake of fairness, we were both using the same score. Although it was the same song, a completely different sound flowed through the halls of the manor. Everyone there, me included, collectively held our breaths as we listened to the amazing performance. I'd always thought he was just a spoiled, stuck-up prince, but it turned out that he had an amazing talent!

At the end of his performance all the servants burst into applause, which didn't happen after I'd played.

"Amazing! Prince Alan, that was really amazing!" I burst out. I was pretty tone-deaf, but even I could tell a great performance apart from an average one.

Yet Alan himself didn't seem pleased; he had a hard expression on his face. "...It's no big deal."

"That's not true! You have an amazing talent!"

"...I don't have anything that deserves to be called a talent."

The more I praised him, the harder his features became. *What's wrong with him?*

"As Katarina said, that was most impressive," Jeord said, praising his twin's performance.

"…But you don't really think that, do you?" Alan muttered. His expression was pained, like the one I saw earlier. Suddenly he shouted, "What is this, pity? I don't need it! To you, I'm nothing but a failure! I'm worthless!" Then, as if running away from something, he bolted straight out of the room.

While I had no idea what was going on, I felt like such a dramatic escape needed an equally dramatic pursuit. Ignoring the stunned expressions of the servants, I chased after Alan like the heroine in a *shoujo* manga.

Apparently it was true that people instinctively ran away to familiar places. Alan was standing under the same trees where we'd held out contests. He looked up at me slightly as I approached, but he didn't seem relieved at all. He just hung his head again.

"…Have you come to laugh at me too?" Alan demanded.

"Huh?" I had no idea what he meant. *What am I supposed to be laughing at? Nothing seems funny to me.*

"…You're here to laugh, aren't you? 'Don't think you're all that just because you can play the piano'… something like that, right?"

"…What do you mean, 'just' because you can play the piano? That's no 'just'! You have an incredible talent!" After witnessing such an amazing performance, I would have thought that Alan would at least be a little proud of himself. I definitely hadn't expected him to get all modest.

Now that I heard his magnificent playing, I couldn't help but compare it to my own performance. When I thought about it now, my self-assessment dropped from "acceptable" to "not good at all."

"I don't need your pity, Katarina. I'm worthless, after all. I'm just what's left behind after Jeord takes all the glory."

I had assumed that Alan was haughty and proud, but apparently he was really negative about himself.

"It's not pity! Prince Alan, why is it that you have so little confidence in yourself?"

"Ha. I've been compared to Jeord ever since I was born. I bet Jeord took all the good stuff for himself when we were still in Mother's womb. So if you think about it, how can leftover dregs have any kind of confidence?"

Hmm. Is that what it is? Come to think of it, that was Alan's backstory in *Fortune Lover*. Ever since the day he was born, Alan had been constantly compared to Jeord, and yet could never best his twin brother in anything. No matter how hard Alan worked, Jeord would accomplish whatever he tried to do before he had the chance, all the while remaining cool and collected.

I guess just telling Alan, who's been dealing with this all his life, to suddenly have confidence in himself and work hard would be pretty insensitive. It was Mary, Alan's cute fiancée, who had healed his heart in the events of the game.

It wasn't like Alan was a failure. In the game, Alan's grades in the academy were top-class. The problem here wasn't Alan's capabilities, but rather Jeord being too good at everything he did.

Even so, Alan's performance was really spectacular. It seemed like he had a knack for music. I thought I remembered that he played violin for the protagonist several times in the game. I would guess that Alan could beat Jeord in the subject of music, at least. He definitely had the talent for it. In other words…

"…Personally, I think it is more that each of you have your own particular strengths. Your own… fortes."

"…What do you mean?"

Uh-oh. I accidentally blurted it out! A-And Alan's looking at me now!

"Umm… Well, I think that Prince Jeord has things that he's suited to and good at, but he also has things that he doesn't do well. The same goes for you, Prince Alan. There are skills that you can be proud of too. It's just a matter of… individual strengths and weaknesses." It was a long-winded explanation, but I think I managed to get out what I was trying to say.

"Individual strengths… and weaknesses? So you're saying that even Jeord has something he isn't good at? I've never heard anything like that."

Alan had a point — it seemed like Jeord could do anything without breaking a sweat. Somehow he was as skilled at the sword as he was intelligent, despite the fact that he spent so much of his time visiting my manor. In fact, he recently even offered to help with the harvest, and it turned out he could gather crops faster than I ever could.

Still, there must be something he was bad at or at least had difficulty with. That was what I always thought to myself, until…

"Eheheheh. I know Prince Jeord's weakness…"

"Wha?!"

A bold smile lit up my face. After all, I wasn't making it up. Recently, I had found out the one thing that stopped Jeord in his tracks.

I discovered it completely by accident. I had always thought of Jeord as a picture-perfect prince through and through, with no faults or weaknesses. But when Jeord started helping me with my harvest and we started spending days together out in the fields, I, like the old lady in the neighborhood who knows everyone's secrets, found out his weakness.

"Well… the thing that Prince Jeord absolutely cannot stand is…"

"Is…?" Alan continued staring at me, frozen in surprise and anticipation. On my face was a malicious smile — just like the smile of a villainess.

It happened a few weeks ago. On that day, Jeord and Mary were visiting the manor, planning to take home some of the crops that I had grown. The two of them and Keith offered to help me with the harvest, and that was when *it* appeared.

It darted around by my legs, and then seemed like it was going for Mary. Wanting to stop it from scaring her, I prepared to catch it first. But then it suddenly changed course and made a beeline for Jeord, who was watching warily nearby. And for the first time in my life, I saw the always-calm Jeord panic.

Perhaps the perfect Jeord *did* have a weakness.

Remembering the event with an evil grin still on my face, I spotted Jeord. He had come searching for us, probably because we were taking so long. Until now I was just guessing, but this would be the perfect chance to confirm my theory.

With that thought in mind, I reached into my pocket and grabbed onto something I'd been carrying around with me, hidden, for the past few days. I pulled Alan behind some bushes and we crouched down to hide, watching Jeord until the perfect moment. Then, as Jeord approached our hiding place, I yanked it out of my pocket and tossed it at his feet.

"Uwaargh?!" A strangled cry rose from Jeord's throat at the sight of the sudden object. His normally calm and collected expression was gone, replaced with surprise, confusion, and hesitation.

"Aha, I was right!" I giggled, still hidden in the bushes.

"Hey, hold up... What exactly is his weakness supposed to be? What did you toss at him?" Alan asked, apparently not entirely convinced, so I told him what it was.

"It was a SNAKE!"

"A snake?!"

"Well, it's actually a fake one. It's not like I can keep a real snake in my pocket!"

"...I don't think most people put snakes of any kind in their pockets. Well? Why did you toss it at him?"

"Like I said, I'm showing you Prince Jeord's weakness."

"Weakness... you don't mean?! Is it snakes?!"

"Yes! It was just a hunch at first, but looking at how he just reacted, I can say for sure that he is afraid of snakes!" I declared, swelling with pride at my accomplishment. *This is an amazing discovery. I've finally found the flaw of the picture-perfect prince!*

The "snake" that I had just thrown was a toy, handmade by yours truly from rolled paper. It was a tool that I had made for the sole purpose of discovering Jeord's weakness. Of course it looked nothing like the real thing, but it still had a great effect.

"His weakness is snakes...? He really does look freaked. This isn't the kind of thing I meant, but... snakes, huh? I've never seen him lose it like this."

Alan, who had been muttering to himself all this time, was ignoring the fact that I was so pleased with myself that I could almost break into a victory dance. Jeord's weakness! Now, even if I were confronted with a Catastrophic Bad End, I would have a trump card!

As I practically bounced with excitement, I didn't notice that a dark presence had slowly approached me from behind.

"Katarina... It would seem that you are in a most delightful mood. I wonder what has brought this about?"

"Yikes?!"

Turning around, I came face to face with Jeord, who was standing with a radiant smile on his face. In his hand was the toy snake I had just tossed at him moments ago. *He's smiling so brightly, but for some reason it's... terrifying.* I slowly became aware of a dark aura rising from his being.

"P-Prince Jeord..."

"To think that I was worried about you, since you had gone off chasing after Alan and did not return... What then, may I ask, is this?" Jeord said, holding up the toy snake before my eyes.

"Ah... Um. That... That is... Uh..." I could only stare helplessly, unable to say a single word in the face of Jeord's tremendously intimidating aura. *This is bad! I just wanted to test my theory with a little prank, but now I've got him angry! No, he's completely livid!*

Actually, why is he so sure it was me who threw it when he didn't even see me do it?!

"Katarina... did you not turn nine just this very last month?"

"...Yes."

"Nine years of age, Katarina Claes. The oldest daughter of a Duke, and my very own fiancée... one would think that she would hardly throw a toy like this, yes...?"

"...Ugh."

Jeord's already brilliant smile rapidly intensified.

This... this is true fear. What if I'm exiled from the kingdom for the crime of "assault by projectile snake on His Highness the third prince?"

How could this be?! A Catastrophic Bad End already?!

"Come to think of it, Katarina. I have not met with Madam Claes today. Perhaps you would know of her whereabouts?"

"Oh, um, Mother is having tea with Keith," I said, distracted by the sudden change of subject and answering without thinking.

Jeord continued smiling as he processed my response. "I see. Well then, Katarina. I really should greet her myself. After all, I have much to say to her — on certain peculiar incidents, such as your tree-climbing competitions with Alan, and the fact that you threw this... toy at me."

"Ah?!" *What?! Is Jeord going to sell me out to Mother, just because I sent a projectile toy snake in his general direction?!* As expected of the black-hearted Prince Jeord, an embodiment of true primal fear.

As much as I begged and pleaded with Jeord, who was now marching straight towards Mother, all he did was smile. A radiant, brilliant smile with a shade of malice. *I have angered the black-hearted prince — the one person I shouldn't have crossed!*

Still wallowing in despair as I chased after the fuming Jeord, I heard a faint voice behind me. I looked around and saw that the source was Alan, who I'd forgotten about for a second. He was laughing — hugging his stomach and laughing his heart out explosively as if a dam had burst inside him.

Damn it, Alan! How could you laugh at my misfortune?! I know it's my own fault, but...

But for now, I had bigger problems than Alan. I still needed to chase Jeord down, so I ran after him. Unfortunately, it probably goes without saying that someone like me couldn't possibly subdue Jeord's rage.

That was how Mother found out about my tree-climbing contests with Alan, and about my projectile snake-toss. I ended up having to sit through hours of painful lectures that day.

Looking back on it though, it wasn't a complete disaster — I'd taken a huge step towards my goal by discovering Jeord's weakness. If I ended up in a Catastrophic Bad End where he tried to cut me down with his sword, all I'd have to do is throw a projectile snake and make a run for it while he panicked.

It was a flawless plan. *Katarina Claes, you are an outstanding strategist.* All I had to do was work on improving my projectile snakes from now until I went to the academy. I'd made them more lifelike and convincing, and then make sure to keep one in my pocket at all times! It was an ingenious method of avoiding a Catastrophic Bad End.

After that day, Alan stopped challenging me to any more competitions, but kept coming on visits to Claes Manor. After a while, I realized that he had started talking normally with Jeord, though I didn't know when that had started changing.

Hmm, I wonder why? I was curious, but I didn't have time to think too much about it. I had to prepare myself for the days ahead by taking bold steps towards the creation of a realistic snake. All in the name of defeating Prince Jeord!

I am the fourth-born prince of the kingdom, Alan Stuart. My older twin brother, Jeord, is the third-born prince.

My health was bad for the first few years of my life, and I spent most of my time bedridden. 'Cause of that, my mother and my caretakers took great care of me. I guess you could say they spoiled me.

As I started getting stronger, I eventually reached a point where I could start my physical and academic training. From then on, I worked hard to catch up to my brother. My tutors always praised me, and that made me get a little ahead of myself. It wasn't until I had tutoring sessions with Jeord that I realized how big the difference between us was. While I was racking my brains for an answer to a question, he'd just solve it easily without batting an eye. Our swordplay lessons were the same way. I'd rush at Jeord with all my might, but he'd always deflect my blows easily and would never break a sweat.

I realized that I was inferior to my brother — the difference between us was too big. My teachers always said that Jeord was "special" and that it was natural for me to lose to him. I guess they were trying to comfort me. But it wasn't long before I refused to take any more lessons with him, and started avoiding him completely. I couldn't stand being compared to him or even being around him.

One day, I overheard a conversation.

"Prince Alan is always somewhat lacking, isn't he?"

"I don't think that's his fault — didn't he live the first few years of his life bedridden?"

"Ah, yes, and having that Jeord as a twin brother... the poor thing."

"Maybe all the good bits were taken by Prince Jeord when they were still in their mother's womb!"

"Haha, so you're saying he only got the leftovers?"

"Hey, now, that's a little too much, isn't it?"

The servants spoke with one another, laughing as they strolled through the royal castle's hallways.

I felt like my vision was going dark. I couldn't even muster up any anger at the way they were talking about me.

The words pierced my heart. Especially when they said *"Maybe all the good bits were taken by Prince Jeord!"* Once I heard that, it was like a thorn that I couldn't pull out. I started feeling like everyone was saying the same thing — my tutors, the servants, and everyone else I met.

It didn't matter how hard I tried, Jeord would always tower over me with that cool and collected expression of his. I don't remember when exactly it started, but eventually I was consumed by an inferiority complex.

But even as I tried so hard to do better than him, and paid so much attention to everything he did, Jeord wasn't interested in me at all. It was as if I didn't even exist. It was painful, and it made me feel a deep resentment towards him. And yet, the more distance I put between me and my brother, the more I hated him, the more it hurt inside.

It was in the spring of my eighth birthday that I heard about Jeord's engagement. The castle was full of gossip about it. Apparently he'd decided to take the daughter of a powerful duke as his future bride. A few months after that, my engagement was finalized too. But unlike Jeord, I didn't ask her myself.

Since I was the last prince without a fiancée, all the other nobles had jumped at the opportunity to parade their daughters in front of me. In the end, it was decided that I'd be engaged to the youngest daughter of the Hunt family, Mary Hunt, for political reasons.

Luckily for me, she turned out to be really cute. She looked like a doll with her large, round eyes the color of burnt sienna and long eyelashes to compliment them. It seemed to take a lot of effort for her to greet me with her soft voice. She really was adorable. As the youngest in my family, it felt like I'd suddenly gained a cute little sister of my own.

Eventually, we ended up talking about the garden she'd been taking care of in her manor's courtyard. It really was beautiful. When I told her I thought so, she smiled gently. It reminded me of a book I'd read the day before called *The Girl with the Green Thumb*. The girl in the story had special hands that were good at raising plants and caring for them. A "green thumb." I thought that Mary was the same, so I mentioned it to her, but…

"In truth, I was told a few days ago that I had a green thumb. Special hands, too…"

"…"

It was like someone had read my mind and said it to Mary before me. I lost my train of thought and was left speechless.

"Lady Katarina, who has been most kind to me, mentioned that to me just the day before." Mary seemed different as she talked about it. She was staring into space, looking like a maiden in love.

Meanwhile, I was left in the dust. I could only say "Oh, is that so." But Mary seemed prompted by my short response, as she started talking passionately about this "Lady Katarina."

From that day on, all Mary would talk about was Lady Katarina. When I tried to invite her over for tea, she'd always refuse and say that she had "plans with Lady Katarina." *Who even is this person?!* I thought resentfully. But soon enough, my question was answered.

Katarina Claes was the eldest daughter of Duke Claes… and she was Jeord's fiancée. *Jeord takes everything from me, all with that smug face of his. And now this? His fiancée is going to take Mary away from me?*

I could feel my vision darkening again. Before I knew it, I was already in a carriage to Claes Manor. This Katarina Claes was late, making me wait in the guest parlor, but eventually she showed up and introduced herself. She had azure eyes and brown hair, and was apparently the same age as me. Although I wouldn't call her ugly at all, her eyes slanted upwards, making her look like a severe person.

This was Jeord's fiancée? The beautiful lady that Mary loves so much? I couldn't believe my eyes. *Well, whatever.* I immediately brought up my problem.

"Did you know that Mary Hunt is now my fiancée?"

"Well, yes… I do know that."

I was incensed by the fact that she could say that with a straight face — and so readily, too.

"So you do know. Stop seducing her, then!"

"…S-Seduce?! What?!" Katarina's azure eyes opened wide at my accusation. It was like she was pretending not to know anything about it, which made me even angrier.

"Don't play dumb! Every time I ask her out, she says no! She's all like 'Oh, today I have an appointment with Lady Katarina.' In fact, *you* are all she talks about when she's with me! Mary has a pure heart, so clearly you're at fault for seducing her! There's no other explanation!"

"Wh-What is that supposed to mean?! I'm not going to stand here and listen to this nonsense!" Katarina's slanted eyes seemed to become even sharper, if that was possible.

"What nonsense? This is the truth! With that face of yours, you've corrupted my pure Mary!"

"What is wrong with you?! I've done no such thing! In fact, it's YOUR fault for asking Mary out when she already has plans to visit me! If you were really charming, no girl would turn down your invitation! You're CHARM-LESS! Mary keeps talking about me?! Well of course she would! It's because you're BORING!"

"…Charm-less… Boring…" I was at a loss for words. I'd been treated like Jeord's leftovers for so long, but this was the first time anyone had said something like that to my face. It was just too much — I started laughing in spite of myself.

"…Ha. Haha. This is the first time I've been ridiculed to my face…"

"…Um. That just now was…"

"Prepare yourself, Katarina Claes. I shall take your train of insults as a thrown gauntlet," I said proudly. "I challenge you to a duel!"

…*How did I end up here?* I wondered as I stood in front of a tree.

Yes, I did challenge Katarina Claes to a duel. I felt like we had to settle this by the sword amongst men… but she was a woman, so I let her choose a different kind of challenge. I assumed she'd choose a chess match or something like that, but…

"Tree-climbing," Katarina said without batting an eye.

I had no idea what she meant by that. What was tree-climbing supposed to be? I knew what a tree was, and what climbing was, but I couldn't figure out what she was suggesting. I had never done anything like it in all eight years of my life. Maybe commoner children did it, but noble children climbing trees was unheard of.

Katarina, as if laughing at me, asked, "Are you unable to climb trees, Prince Alan?"

I have to protect my pride as a man! So I answered her without hesitation. "Of course not! I accept your challenge!"

And this was why we were now standing before the two tallest trees in the gardens of Claes Manor, all lined up for our challenge. The rules of the challenge were simple — the first to reach the top of their tree wins. But while the terms were straightforward, I had never climbed a tree in my life before. I didn't even know how it was done.

Still, I had accepted Katarina's challenge, so I had no choice. I steeled myself, rolling up my sleeves.

"Well then, Prince Alan. Are you ready?"

"...Yeah. Right. Anytime."

"We'll begin on the count of three. Anne, my personal maid, will do the honors."

"Y-Yeah."

The challenge started under the watchful gazes of our servants... and then promptly ended. I lost terribly. All I could do was climb to the very first branch of the thing — I mean it's not like I knew how to do it in the first place!

Katarina, on the other hand, was zipping up her tree like some sort of monkey. She was perched all the way at the very top. *Why exactly is the daughter of the Claes family so good at climbing trees? Isn't she the daughter of a duke? Do daughters of dukes usually climb trees?* I couldn't understand this. My thoughts were a jumbled mess.

"We have a clear winner. Can we all move on now?" Katarina said, looking down at me with a smug expression.

She's so full of herself! Before I knew it, I'd already spoken. "Again! I challenge you again! This is the first time I've climbed a tree — I just wasn't used to it!"

"No problem. But don't think you can win so easily, Prince."

"Bring it on!"

However, no matter how hard I tried and how many times I challenged her, Katarina always won. She really was like a monkey. So I decided to delay the challenge and come back a few days later to settle it.

A few weeks passed since I started challenging Katarina Claes. After a few more tree-climbing races, I noticed something interesting: Katarina was always serious. She didn't hold back or give me any slack just because I was a prince. And whenever she looked at me, I felt like she was looking right *into* me.

Up until now, no one had ever challenged me like that, with their heart and soul. No matter how hard I tried, Jeord never even looked at me. I didn't exist in his world.

Katarina's unwavering gaze and sincere attitude caused the aching in my heart to slowly fade away. I looked forward to my visits to Claes Manor. Visiting Katarina was… fun.

But that only lasted until a certain day.

"Jeord?! What are you doing here?!" I exclaimed, shocked by the sight of my brother at Claes Manor.

"You sound as if me being here is a most mysterious thing. This is the home of my fiancée — my presence here is to be expected," Jeord replied, a confident smirk plastered across his face.

He was right, of course, and I couldn't think of a response. *How could I forget that Katarina is my brother's fiancée?* I was surprised at myself.

"…Doesn't matter. I'm here for a challenge with her today. Don't get in the way."

"About those challenges... I heard that you have failed to achieve victory, time and time again. Would it not be best to simply give up...?" Jeord said, his eyes cold.

"Maybe all the good bits were taken by Prince Jeord!" I could hear those words echoing in my head again.

"...No! NO! We still need to settle it! I can win this! I... I know I can...!"

Don't look down on me! Don't make a fool of me! My vision clouded. My surroundings were sinking into darkness. I had almost forgotten about the heavy pain I carried in my chest since it had become so light and warm these past few weeks. *No... This is bad. I don't feel good at all...*

"...Um, Prince Alan," Katarina called out to me. "If you don't mind, maybe we could change the terms of the challenge? If we keep climbing trees my mother will eventually find out, and she'll be really mad." She had a strange expression on her face. She seemed strangely cheerful, but her smile was twitching a little.

The pain faded a little at the sight of her face. With her suggestion, our tree-climbing race was called off and replaced with a musical competition. We'd be playing piano against each other.

After moving to the music room, we began our contest. Katarina was up first, playing a practice song meant for children and beginners. She made a few mistakes, but she kept playing until the end.

Next was my turn. When I was done, everyone in the room clapped. Katarina, in fact, seemed the most excited out of everyone. She was jumping, clapping, and even cheering.

"Amazing! Prince Alan, that was really amazing!" she said, praising me just like the tutors back at the castle. She must have been pitying me.

"…It's no big deal."

"That's not true! You have an amazing talent!"

"…I don't have anything that deserves to be called a talent." It was true that playing musical instruments came easier to me than academics or swordplay, but… *A talent? Me? No. There's no way I could have anything like that.*

I was the leftovers after Jeord had taken away all the good bits for himself. No matter what I did, I would never do better than him.

"As Katarina said, that was most impressive," Jeord said, with that fake smile he always had on his smug face. He, who could do anything, was making fun of me. I knew he was.

My vision started fading again. The pain that had faded now back in full force, stabbing into my heart.

"…But you don't really think that, do you? What is this, pity? I don't need it! To you, I'm nothing but a failure! I'm worthless!"

I couldn't stand it any longer! I couldn't stand to be in the same place as Jeord! I felt like everyone was just laughing at me.

I ran out of the room as fast as my legs would go. I ran, sprinting into the darkness. I wanted to just disappear, but instead found myself standing by the trees Katarina and I had climbed.

After standing there for a while, I felt someone arrive. I raised my head, thinking that a servant had come to check on me, but it was Katarina.

"…Have you come to laugh at me too?" I blurted out.

"Huh?"

"…You're here to laugh, aren't you? 'Don't think you're all that just because you can play the piano'… something like that, right?"

"…What do you mean, 'just' because you can play the piano? That's no 'just'! You have an incredible talent!"

"I don't need your pity, Katarina. I'm worthless, after all. I'm just what's left behind after Jeord takes all the glory."

I'd thought that Katarina was different from all those people in the castle. But in the end she was the same as them, with their pointless pity and encouragement. I knew that they were laughing at me from the shadows.

After all, I knew how useless and ordinary I was. That was how it had always been, and what they had always said about me.

"It's not pity! Prince Alan, why is it that you have so little confidence in yourself?"

"Ha. I've been compared to Jeord ever since I was born. I bet Jeord took all the good stuff for himself when we were still in Mother's womb. So if you think about it, how can leftover dregs have any kind of confidence?" I said, loathing myself. Now, even Katarina would just stand there and say nothing, just like everyone else.

"...Personally, I think it is more that each of you have your own particular strengths. Your own... fortes." Katarina, however, did not stand still and remain silent.

"...What do you mean?" I muttered, glaring straight at her.

"Umm... Well, I think that Prince Jeord has things that he's suited to and good at, but he also has things that he doesn't do well. The same goes for you, Prince Alan. There are skills that you can be proud of too. It's just a matter of... individual strengths and weaknesses."

"Individual strengths... and weaknesses? So you're saying that even Jeord has something he isn't good at? I've never heard anything like that."

Look at his smug face, and his confident, cool expression. Jeord can do anything he wants. Even his taste in food is perfect! I've never heard complaints that Jeord is picky with his meals.

139

That's how perfect he is. Prince Jeord is good at everything... unlike me.

But then...

"Eheheheh. I know Prince Jeord's weakness..."

"Wha?!"

A confident smile spread across Katarina's face. "Well... the thing that Prince Jeord absolutely cannot stand is..."

"Is...?"

I gulped as I waited and watched. *There he is.* Jeord had wandered close by, searching for the two of us. Katarina, seeing her target, suddenly pulled something out of her pocket and tossed it at my brother.

"Uwaargh?!"

That mystery object landed in front of Jeord, and he let out a weird sound. I had never seen him look so panicked before.

"Hey, hold up..." I said. "What exactly is his weakness supposed to be? What did you toss at him?" Jeord was completely freaking out. What was it? I had to know!

Katarina answered my question with a smug expression. "It was a SNAKE!"

"A snake?!" I was completely stunned.

"Well, it's actually a fake one. It's not like I can keep a real snake in my pocket!"

"...I don't think most people put snakes of any kind in their pockets. Well? Why did you toss it at him?"

"Like I said, I'm showing you Prince Jeord's weakness."

"Weakness... you don't mean?! Is it snakes?!"

"Yes! It was just a hunch at first, but looking at how he just reacted, I can say for sure that he is afraid of snakes!" Katarina declared triumphantly. For some reason, she seemed really proud of her discovery.

But… Jeord is afraid of snakes? I never would have guessed.

Actually, that's not what I wanted to know! I wanted to know what I could beat Jeord at. I thought maybe he was bad at some kind of sword technique or academic subject? But… snakes?

Even so, he really does look intimidated. Look at him!

This was completely unexpected. Prince Jeord, the respected prince of the great kingdom, afraid of a toy snake thrown by Katarina Claes?

At that point, I had to take back what I thought. Katarina Claes was *definitely* different from the people at the castle. *Completely different from any other noble kid.*

"Ha. Haha…" *She's really something else! What a crazy girl!*

While I was lost in my thoughts, Katarina was caught in the act by Jeord. My brother was definitely angry. You could see it in his eyes, and from how Katarina was slowly backing away. But actually… it seemed to me like he wasn't actually angry, but just playing the part to mess with Katarina.

The Jeord I knew always seemed bored and had a fake smile on his face. He was uninterested in other people, or anything really. But I had just seen him genuinely panicking at the sight of Katarina's toy snake. And now, he was angry because of it…? *Is this really Jeord…?*

I could only stare blankly as Jeord announced his plan to tell Madam Claes about all the things Katarina had done. Katarina, who had been so confident and triumphant a second ago, now seemed pale and shaken. I didn't really get why she was so proud in the first place, though.

Look at her! She was now desperately apologizing to Jeord, looking like she could cry. While I did feel kinda bad for her, I couldn't help but laugh. *This is ridiculous! Katarina, Jeord… they both look so silly!*

I couldn't hold it in any longer. I doubled over, hugging my stomach, and laughed. Tears flowed from my eyes, but I kept laughing. It was the first time in my life I had laughed like this. I wasn't sure whether I was laughing or crying anymore. The tears I'd never let myself cry were mixed with new tears of laughter and joy. After a while, my vision cleared and my heart felt at ease.

Katarina was forcibly escorted away by Madam Claes, so Jeord and I returned to the royal castle.

I called out to Jeord with a laugh. "Ha! Even you have something you can't deal with, huh?"

Before I knew it, I was talking with Jeord casually. Come to think of it, it had been a long time since I'd talked to him at all. Jeord's usual smug smile faltered, replaced with a scowl. It was the first time I had seen him make another expression.

"I would not say that I cannot deal with it. It is more of... something I do not like very much."

For some reason, Jeord couldn't maintain his usual smile when the subject of snakes came up. *He's really that freaked out by snakes? That's hilarious! I can't believe even my brother has a side like that.*

"I used to think nothing could faze you. I thought you could do anything."

After hearing all the malicious gossip, I thought of Jeord as someone much more menacing than he really was. All this time, I hadn't been seeing the real Jeord. Even he had weaknesses, and I was the same. I realized that important fact... all thanks to that crazy daughter of Duke Claes.

"Of course there are things I am bad at and things I cannot do."

"Oh, really? Tell me." Encouraged by the half-scowl smile that Jeord still had on his face, I casually continued the conversation.

"Ah, yes... well. For example, predicting the actions of a certain Katarina Claes, I would say?"

"...Yeah. That makes sense," I replied, smiling awkwardly myself.

Climbing trees out of nowhere with the speed of a monkey, and then suddenly hurling toy snakes at people? Even the great Jeord couldn't get a handle on someone like that.

Katarina's triumphant face appeared in my mind — that face she made after she startled Jeord with the toy snake...

My cheeks felt warm. I wanted to remember that face for a while, and remember how absurd it all was.

"On another note... did you not have yet another challenge with Katarina today? Are you going to challenge her again soon?"

"Hmm... Yeah. About that... I think we're good."

I was done with these challenges. All this time, I'd thought the most important thing was winning, but now it seemed like a distant lie I had told myself. A sense of peace had come over me.

"In that case, we should never meet at Claes Manor again."

"Huh? What? Why?" I said, suddenly jolted back to my senses. I didn't understand what he meant.

"Why? But of course, now that you are done with your challenges, there is no further need to visit, no?"

"Well... I guess that's true..." I had only been visiting Claes Manor to compete with Katarina. Now that there wouldn't be any more contests, I didn't have a reason to go anymore...

I could picture Katarina's azure eyes staring straight at me. Even if she was my brother's fiancée, not visiting Claes Manor anymore meant that I wouldn't see Katarina again. At least, not often.

...I didn't like that idea.

As I stood, lost in thought, Jeord suddenly looked straight at me, his expression determined and serious. It was the first time I had seen him look like that.

"She is my fiancée, Alan."

"Huh?" *What's that supposed to mean? I know that already!*

"Ah, so you do not realize it yourself. Regardless, brother… I will never let you have her," Jeord said, with his smug smile returning. He quickly turned and was gone, swiftly walking towards his room.

I didn't really get his point. All I could do was watch as he disappeared down the hallway. Up until now the sight of him would have filled my heart with pain, but for some reason I felt fine now. It wasn't that I was fond of him, but the black aura that had haunted my vision was gone.

I headed back to my room too. On my way there, I looked out of a window. There in the garden were two tall trees, standing side by side. It made me think of that strange daughter of a duke who was ridiculously good at climbing trees.

Was she sad after being scolded by Madam Claes? I was the one who had challenged her in the first place, so I felt kinda responsible.

Well, I suppose I could just visit and apologize. Maybe I could bring some of those treats that she loved so much. She'd stuff her face full of them like a squirrel.

Just thinking about it is hilarious. I feel better already.

It was now the second summer since I had retrieved the memories of my past life, and I was ten years old.

At around this time last year, my crops had been facing a wilting crisis and Alan had been challenging me over and over. But this year was turning out to be a lot more peaceful.

Alan and Mary were now following in the footsteps of my fiancé, Prince Jeord, and were coming for regular visits to Claes Manor. Although the two brothers didn't seem to get along very well at first, now they seemed to be fine with each other. Alan had started to seriously practice the piano and violin, putting a lot of effort into studying music. People started noticing his talent and calling him a musical genius who was blessed by the gods.

Mary had changed a lot too. She was timid when I first met her, but now she was a confident young noble lady. Despite that, she still somehow looked up to me. In fact, just the other day she said something really bold with a dizzy look in her eyes. It was something like "If I were a man myself, I would very well take Lady Katarina as my bride!" *What a sweet girl!*

In response, I said "Well, Prince Alan is your fiancé. Shouldn't you spend time with him?" But Mary said swiftly, "I refuse, as that would mean I would have less time to spend with you, Lady Katarina." It was such a merciless refusal that I was at a loss for words.

Even my cute brother, Keith, was living an active and social life instead of being locked up in his room. Of course, I didn't want him to become a playboy and end up taking advantage of all the ladies around him. So I reminded him constantly to be kind and gentle to women, and I think it was working.

I had also been working on improving my Catastrophic Bad Ending avoidance strategies, mainly focusing on how I could escape from Jeord if he ever came at me with a sword. I trained hard at my swordplay and footwork until my tutor was glowing with pride. My old weakness was gone!

Plus, I had one more trick up my sleeve now. The head gardener of Claes Manor, "Grandpa" Tom, was really handy with his tools. With his advice, my toy snakes became even more lifelike. When Jeord saw one, he'd definitely think it's the real thing. In fact, they were so lifelike that I could probably sell them at a marketplace. Another way I could cope with exile if that ever happened.

I hadn't been slacking off in the magic department either — after all, it was my plan to be able to make a living with magic if I needed to. It had only been a year since I'd started working with a magic tutor, and my Dirt Bump spell had made a lot of progress. It had improved from a lump of two or three centimeters to small earth hedges of around fifteen centimeters tall. If I kept going at the same rate, I'd have to change the name. Maybe something like "Rise, Wall of Earth!"

My brother Keith had also made good progress, and could now completely control his own magic. In fact, even a golem the size of the one that sent me flying was now totally obedient to him. Encouraged by his success, I tried to manipulate an Earth Golem too. But the infusion of magic into a golem was surprisingly difficult, and it turned out to be way beyond me.

146

Since I was reincarnated as the noble daughter of a duke, I'd assumed that I'd be born with more capabilities than I'd had in my previous life. But unfortunately, it seemed like not much had changed. My magic tutor reminded me often that you needed to have a strong mana capacity to use magic properly. It really was a deeply complicated subject.

The days went by, and my life was carefree, but fulfilling. I even developed a new hobby on top of tilling the fields and climbing trees. It was... reading. Of course, I don't mean books on history or economics or anything difficult like that. The books I liked were romance novels.

Even though they were usually talked about in hushed tones and whispers, a romance novel boom was sweeping across the nearby towns. Novels like that were supposed to be beneath a noble's tastes because of their "vulgar" nature, but I read them anyway in private.

How did I end up with these kinds of books in the first place? It was thanks to a particular maid in the manor. For one reason or another, she had a good understanding of the trends in the streets of town. All it took was her loaning me one book, and I was hooked. I guess that makes sense, since I needed a replacement for the manga and anime I'd so voraciously enjoyed in my past life.

There were lots of different kinds of stories — love stories about charming princes, or even beautiful stories of friendship. While there weren't nearly as many different options in the market as I had access to in my previous life, I took to them like a fish to water. My current favorite was a story about a beautiful friendship between two girls, a princess and a commoner girl. It was called *Princess Emerald and Sophia*.

I was ecstatic when Mother quickly approved of my newfound hobby and handed me some allowance to buy the books. According to Anne, the reason was that "it would be far more appropriate for a young lady to quietly read books in her room, as opposed to getting up to no good outside." Well, at least now I could buy as many books as I wanted!

But amidst all this good news, there was one disappointment: the maid who'd introduced me to these novels in the first place left the manor because she was getting married. When she left, I lost a friend and comrade, and now had no one to talk about romance novels with.

It drove me crazy! I really wanted to share my passion with someone else. In search of a kindred spirit, I even tried to introduce the books to Anne and Mary, but they weren't interested. It was such a bummer.

Ah, I want a friend! I really do! I'll have to go looking for one at the next tea party.

Actually, Jeord and Alan were planning to hold a tea party at the royal castle in a few days. Since it was hosted by royalty, there should be lots of young lords and ladies. With such a high number of people, I might be able to find someone who truly understood my passion.

Before I knew it, I actually started looking forward to the royal tea party. It would be held in a corner of the royal gardens — a very wide corner, considering how large the grounds were. It would be similar to the one I attended at the Hunt manor, a practice event for the social dance parties we'd attend once we all came of age.

Naturally, though, this royal event was larger and grander than any I'd been to before. It was on a totally different scale, and there were a lot more people there. Since I normally spent a lot of time with Jeord and Alan, it would be strange to only exchange brief pleasantries with them. Since they were hosting the event, they wouldn't have time for our usual long conversations.

Having learned my lesson from my first tea party misadventure, I planned on sitting still and drinking my tea as elegantly as I could rather than stuffing my face. But of course, as you'd expect from the royal kitchens, the tea and snacks were unbelievably good. I couldn't even count all the different kinds of food on display!

Resisting temptation was harder than I thought. I tried to be strategic by limiting myself to one of each kind of snack, but I didn't expect to see such a wide variety of teas. I was curious about the rare blends, so I sampled every single one, and soon realized that I'd had a little too much. I could hear swashing in my stomach.

But I had grown as a noble lady, so I excused myself as elegantly as I could and left Mary and Keith behind as I slowly and calmly went to search for the nearest bathroom before the problem got too urgent.

Then, as I was quickly crossing the castle grounds in search of relief, I ran into something terrifying. It was a vicious dog, running free and unchained. Probably a guard dog that had escaped from its keeper.

I was no good with dogs. They always seemed to hate me for some reason, even in my past life. They'd fly into a rage whenever they saw me, like I was their natural enemy: the monkey. And now the escaped guard dog was baring its fangs at me threateningly. *But we just met seconds ago! What the heck!*

Of course, the unchained dog made a beeline for me. While I could have scared away some kinds of dogs, specifically of the Chihuahua-class, this one was as large as a Doberman. I had no chance against it.

I hiked up my dress and ran as fast as I could, looking for an escape. Since it was me, I of course ended up climbing up a nearby tree. Now that it couldn't reach me from my perch in the tree's branches, the dog howled and growled for what seemed like forever. Eventually, a voice called out for it, probably its master who had noticed the hound was missing. Obeying the voice, the dog turned and left. And then everything was quiet and still.

Relieved, I started making my way downwards, only to see a group of people standing there who I'd never seen before. There were six or seven of them, and apparently they'd decided to start a conversation right at the bottom of the tree I'd climbed.

If I go down now, they'll see that I've been climbing trees! The daughter of a Duke, climbing trees in the royal castle gardens? If word of this gets out, it'll be really bad. I have to get out of here!

But I was at my limit. I already needed to go to the bathroom, and then I was chased by a rabid dog, and ended up climbing a tree. There was only so much strain my bladder could take. Even if climbing down the tree would cause rumors, I didn't have a choice. *It'll be better than peeing myself! Especially at this age!*

Steeling myself, I slid down the tree at full speed. The gathered people stared at me blankly, shocked by my sudden appearance.

"Do excuse me, but you're in my way," I said to the small crowd that had assembled here for apparently no reason. It was as if they'd been placed there by some kind of cruel god for the sole purpose of preventing me from going to the bathroom. My panicked voice came out sterner than I'd planned, sounding cold and demeaning. But now wasn't the time to worry about something like that!

The children scattered like leaves in the wind, apparently terrified of me. *Was I that fearsome? They don't have to run away like that!* But then I realized that there was one girl who was still standing there, possibly too stunned to escape. She had her back to the tree I'd come from and didn't seem to have seen my dramatic entrance.

As she turned around, I was taken aback by how breathtakingly beautiful the girl was. She had crimson eyes and snow-white hair, and stunningly smooth, fair skin that was almost translucent. I was momentarily entranced by her beauty, only to be rudely brought back to reality by the intense pressure in my bladder. If I didn't make it to the bathroom soon, I'd have a true tragedy on my hands.

Using all of my willpower, I managed to smile as gently as I could at the frightened girl, trying to reassure her that I meant no harm. Then I turned and rushed off in search of the bathroom.

By some stroke of luck, I eventually made it and prevented the tea-party tragedy that was looming over me. The worst was over, but I couldn't shake the feeling that one day I wasn't going to be as lucky. From now on, I'd have to seriously consider carrying a portable toilet of some kind whenever I went to a tea party. I thought about that for a while with a serious expression on my otherwise relieved face.

Now that I had taken care of business, I returned to where I was originally sitting at the tea party, only to find that Keith and Mary were gone. They'd been swallowed by the crowds somewhere. Feeling grumpy from being left on my own, I vented my frustration by stuffing whatever leftover snacks I could reach into my mouth.

"Ah… Um." A small voice drifted out from behind me. Turning around, I came face to face with the stunningly beautiful girl whom I had met at the tree.

"Oh, you were the one from just now…"

"Y-Yes. That is correct…" the beautiful girl said, nodding slowly.

The more I looked at her, the more breathtaking she was. I was used to being around beautiful people thanks to Prince Jeord and my other friends, but this girl was in a class of her own. I swallowed hard in spite of myself.

Her pure-white hair looked like strands of silk, cascading in a silent, frozen waterfall. Her skin reminded me of freshly-fallen snow — impossibly pure and soft. And her pale features made her crimson eyes stand out even more as they stared straight into my soul. She reminded me of a character in a romance novel.

Actually... *AH! That's right! She reminds me of Sophia, from that trending novel* Princess Emerald and Sophia*!* In that book, the character of Sophia was a commoner. She had black, silky hair and equally black eyes. Her skin was white like snow. She was a true beauty, and the princess who had sneaked into town was captivated by her.

The girl before me was like the incarnation of Sophia herself. But unlike the character, she was here, right in front of me. I stared at the girl, unable to comprehend what I was seeing.

"Um... a-about just now..." Her snow-white cheeks were now flushed, a gentle shade of red slowly spreading through her face.

This is just like that scene! Just like how Sophia reacts when she first sees Princess Emerald! Unfortunately for the girl, I was no beautiful princess, but instead Katarina Claes, villainess extraordinaire with a face to match.

From what I remembered in the book, the princess said this to Sophia: "What pretty hair you have. Just like strands of silk... Would you mind if I ran my fingers through it, just ever so slightly?"

"...Ah?!" The girl seemed shocked. Her expression was enough to wake me up from my daydream.

Ugh! What have I done? My fantasies slipped out from my lips!

The girl shifted her weight from one leg to another, apparently in a state of panic. A natural reaction if confronted by a fairy-tale princess, of course. But the person who said it to her was me, with my villainess-like face! If I were her, I'd be really scared!

"Ah... Um. I meant to say..." I desperately searched for an excuse.

The panicked girl, however, suddenly blurted out a line of her own. "...Princess Emerald."

WHAT?! Could this possibly be?!

Before I could stop myself, I gripped her shoulders, moving my face close to hers. "Princess Emerald! From the romance novels! M-Maybe! You know of *Princess Emerald and Sophia* too?!"

Intimidated by my sudden approach and the fact that I was gripping her by the shoulders, the girl nodded rapidly, still panicking. Encouraged, I listed off a bunch of titles, only to have the girl nod at each and every single one of them.

I can't believe it! I've found her! My comrade-in-arms in romance novel appreciation!

That's not all! Just like the character in the story, she's also stunningly beautiful!

I am overcome with emotion! With gratitude!

I stood, shivering in place.

"...What are you doing, Big Sister?" It was a familiar, yet suspicious-sounding voice. Turning in the direction of the voice, I was greeted by Keith, who was flanked by Mary.

"...Hm? What do you..." I turned back to the girl and realized what I'd been doing. I had grabbed onto her with my hands, one on each shoulder. My face was close to hers, and my nostrils were flared with excitement.

Oh. I look like a classic pervert.

"Wah! I-I apologize," I said, promptly letting the girl go. I could feel surprised stares turning on me from all directions. *I got so excited that I lost control... I'm really sorry.*

Actually, I don't even know her name! And I didn't tell her mine! I really messed up. I should be disqualified as a noble lady!

I lifted up my dress as elegantly as I could and curtsied while I gave her a formal greeting. "I do apologize for my manners. I am Katarina Claes. Very pleased to make your acquaintance."

Despite the fact that she had been captured by a suspicious-looking villainess, and was now being formally greeted by her, the girl greeted me in return like the noble lady she was.

"...Sophia Ascart."

What?! She's... Sophia? Like the Sophia in the book? Was Sophia based off this beautiful girl?! My literary excitement was off the charts.

"Lady Sophia! If it would please you, would you like to speak in greater detail with me?" I asked enthusiastically, grasping Sophia's hands in my own.

Keith, who had been standing next to me, immediately stepped in. "Big Sister, I do apologize for interrupting you in the midst of such a spirited conversation... but the tea party has already ended. We should make the appropriate preparations and return to the manor."

"Huh?!"

WHAT?! B-But my passionate discussions on novels! We've barely started!

In that case...!

"Well then, Lady Sophia. If you would like, please feel free to pay a visit to Claes Manor."

"...Ah? Um..."

Grasping Sophia's hands once again, I asked her emphatically to come visit me, and was elated when she accepted. *Yesss!* Not wanting to waste the opportunity, I decided on a date and time for the visit on the spot.

"Well then, I will be eagerly awaiting your arrival." Grinning widely, I saw goodbye to Sophia and turned to return to the manor with Keith.

And so, just as I'd hoped, I met a romance novel comrade at the royal tea party. Not only would she discuss my favorite books with me, but she even looked like a character from my favorite book! What a huge success!

I had a huge smile on my face all the way back in the carriage as Keith looked on with a mystified expression.

Soon the promised day came. Sophia turned up for her visit to Claes Manor, which I'd been looking forward to all morning.

"Young miss, the Lady Sophia you had been speaking about has arrived, but..." Anne, apparently here to inform me of Sophia's arrival, seemed a little off.

This is it! Sophia is here! In my hurry to see her I dashed out of the room, leaving Anne with a brief "Thanks!"

As expected, Sophia was waiting for me in the guest parlor. *Beautiful as always... but oh?* For some reason, there was another person there with her.

It was a handsome boy. With his raven-black hair and eyes, he looked very different from Sophia. But now that I looked at them side by side, I could see that their faces looked similar, like they were in the same family. They stood side by side like dolls, perfectly complementing each other. This was probably why Anne was so surprised earlier. Entranced by their beauty, I stared at them in wonder.

The boy called out to me first. "Thank you very much for extending an invitation to my sister. My sister seldom ventures out on her own, so I have come with her. My name is Nicol. I am Sophia's brother."

My hunch turned out to be right — the impossibly handsome boy was Sophia's brother. I was surprised by what he said, thinking that Sophia must be really sheltered. I mean, I wasn't one to talk. I was sheltered in my own way since Mother kept insisting that I have Keith with me at all times and listen to whatever he said. As two noble, sheltered girls, I was sure we'd be friends in no time.

I curtsied properly, first to Sophia's brother and then to her. "No, the pleasure is all mine. Thank you for coming. I am Katarina Claes."

"Nicol Ascart, elder brother of Sophia Ascart. Pleased to make your acquaintance," he said, introducing himself again.

I froze. Nicol Ascart was a name I knew. I'd heard it somewhere before. "Ah, excuse my ignorance, but would you happen to be Chancellor Ascart's son...?"

"Yes. That is correct."

No way?! This person is a potential love interest in Fortune Lover! *No wonder he's so handsome!*

Honestly speaking, I wanted to drop everything and return to my room immediately so I could pull out the strategy guide and give it a good read. That wasn't exactly something I could do right now though, so I did my best to remember the details.

Nicol Ascart... son of Chancellor Ascart, and a childhood friend of Alan and Jeord. A year older than the protagonist, and an upperclassman in the academy. Famous for saying relatively little.

Hmm. That's all I can remember right now. I mean, I didn't get around to trying Nicol's route before I died! I was planning to do it after finishing Jeord's.

I didn't know much about Nicol's route, since I hadn't ever touched it. If my friend hadn't told me about the character, I never would have heard of him at all! She had cleared his route and was telling me all about it.

Let's see… according to what Acchan said, the rival character in Nicol's route is… That's right! His sister!

Yes, I remember now! Nicol is hopelessly overprotective of his sister… and so Sophia is the rival in this case.

To successfully romance Nicol, you have to first make friends with Sophia. I remember Acchan saying something like that.

Ah, thank you so much, Acchan. And I'm also very sorry for getting upset about the spoilers. Who would think that Acchan's spoilers would end up being so helpful?

So… if the rival is indeed Sophia, that would mean that Katarina has nothing to do with it! There are no Catastrophic Bad Ends with Nicol! Also, there won't be any memorable lines for me to accidentally steal, like what happened with Alan and Mary.

Okay then! There should be no problems with me being friends with Sophia. She can be my comrade-in-arms in the enjoyment of romance novels! I won't let her escape!

"…Um. Lady Katarina…?"

Apparently I had gotten lost in my fantasies again. Before I knew it, Sophia was looking straight at me with her pretty face colored with worry.

"Oh, Lady Sophia. I do apologize. It is so nice to see you again! If you would like, I would like to continue our previous conversation…"

I invited Sophia to a table that I'd had prepared with tea and snacks, and we then spent the next few hours getting to know each other. She seemed reserved and even fearful at first, maybe because she was somewhere she wasn't used to. But then she opened up once the conversation shifted to books.

Sophia really did love books. And she didn't just real romance novels — she also read fairy tales and myths, historical fiction, and all kinds of other genres. It was a really interesting conversation, and she even gave me a few recommendations!

The only thing that bothered me a little was that Sophia's brother Nicol hardly spoke at all. In fact, he didn't take part in our discussion at all, instead just watching quietly. I felt bad for excluding him while we were having our cheerful girl-talk, and wondered if I should have called Keith here to keep him company. He really was quiet, just like his character in the game. *What a waste for such a handsome guy to be so quiet!*

Time passed quickly without either of us noticing. Eventually, we were both brought back to reality by one of Sophia's entourage, who whispered that it was almost time for them to return.

Sophia quickly stood up, and her hair glittered and shone in the light. I watched, entranced. *It's really beautiful. It would definitely feel like silk. Would she mind if I touched it, just a little?*

"What beautiful hair you have… Would you mind if I ran my fingers through it, just ever so slightly?" The words escaped before I could catch myself. I had blurted out a line from *Princess Emerald and Sophia*, as if I were the princess herself.

In the novel, Sophia was blushing sweetly. But now…

"…Ack?!"

What a disaster! I've definitely freaked her out! She looks completely scared! What have you done now, Katarina Claes?!

I liked to play with Mary's soft, wavy hair, but I hadn't thought about the fact that touching another noble lady's hair in this world was probably extremely weird. Mary always seemed glad, but still…

To make things worse, the first time I met her I grabbed her by the shoulders and breathed into her face! She must think I'm some kind of deviant!

This is terrible! I can't do anything about this villainess face, but at least I don't want to be branded a pervert! Anything but that!

"…U-Um… well…" I stood rooted to the spot, internally panicking as I searched for an excuse.

"…you?"

"…Huh?"

Sophia had spoken with a weak and quivering voice. I asked her to repeat herself, and…

"…Does it not… disgust you?" Sophia said, in a louder voice now.

Disgust? Disgust… you? Me? Wait! Is she disgusted by my perverse actions?!

No, no Sophia! You have it all wrong, I'm not a pervert at all! Okay, so maybe there was that time a year ago when I supposedly seduced Mary away from a certain haughty prince, but I don't swing that way! I'm normal! I'm just a normal girl!!

"A-About that, I… uh…" *An excuse! Think of one, quickly! Do it now!*

"…Are you not disgusted by my appearance, Lady Katarina?"

I stood, gaping, having lost all my words and the train of thought behind them. *Huh? What? The disgusting one here isn't me… but Sophia? What?*

Sophia continued, looking close to tears, as I stood with my mouth still agape like a gasping goldfish.

"…Does it not disgust you, Lady Katarina? This… hair of mine, white as an elderly woman… And these blood-red eyes. Everyone calls me a disgusting, cursed child."

"Huh?!"

WHAT?! How can something so beautiful be disgusting?! So far in this world, I had seen hair and eyes that were blonde, silver, brown, red, and black. So I'd just assumed that Sophia's white hair and red eyes were normal. *But I guess she's shunned for it? That doesn't make any sense.*

"…Cursed? What do you mean…?"

159

Sophia opened her mouth to speak, but Nicol jumped in and explained coldly. "Malicious rumors. From certain individuals who are jealous of our family's achievements. Such jealousy causes them to spread these baseless accusations."

That made some sense; the Ascarts were a formidable family. I supposed it was only natural for the strong and capable to have enemies, and of course, these enemies would spread nasty rumors about them.

This was true even for the Claes family. While Keith was an accomplished young man and I was a perfectly respectable noble lady, rumors on the street claimed that we were "strange and eccentric." *Definitely baseless. Jealousy is a terrible thing.*

"...Even so. It does little to change the fact that my appearance is disgusting and revolting," Sophia said, with a surprising amount of conviction. She must have heard many of these rumors whispered around her.

But even though I'd never seen anyone like her before, I said truthfully, "Well I think you're really pretty."

"...Ah?" Sophia's eyes opened wide. She stared straight at me— no, *into* me, as I kept talking.

"I think your silky white hair is beautiful. I think your ruby-red, sparkling eyes are beautiful. I think... you... are beautiful."

Now that I've made myself clear, maybe I'll stop seeming like a pervert! No pervert labels for me! I can't handle both this villainess face and the title of a pervert!

Don't worry, Sophia. I'm normal. Definitely normal. Trying to reassure her, I have her my warmest possible smile. "Actually, I would be so pleased if you would come and visit again! And if you don't mind... would you like to be my friend?"

I held out my hands, and was pleasantly surprised when Sophia grasped them in her own. Her beautiful white hands were holding mine tightly. She didn't look surprised or shocked anymore.

That was how I made my very first romance novel-appreciating friend.

I saw Sophia and her entourage out to the porch and waved as they boarded their carriage. Immediately after, I returned to my room and pulled out the "*Fortune Lover* Unofficial Strategy Guide." As expected, there weren't many details recorded there about Nicol.

While I was surprised when I realized that Sophia was a rival character just like Katarina, I hadn't done anything weird this time to mess things up. I felt a wave of relief wash over me. In fact, I was happy. Sophia was the same age as Katarina, and could also use magic. That meant that we'd be in the same year at the magic academy. We'd be able to discuss romance novels even in class!

Overcome with happiness, I jumped up and down on my bed, which of course earned me a stern warning from Anne.

From then on, Sophia started coming on regular visits to Claes Manor — along with Nicol, her silent brother.

Maybe because of Sophia and our passionate conversations, Mary started showing some interest too. She eventually asked to borrow a book, and before long, she joined our little novel appreciation group and made our conversations even more lively.

Sophia had never played outside much before, so I decided to take her out to the fields. In fact, she even started helping me with my crops! While they were both surprised at first, Sophia and Nicol started to get used to me, and eventually didn't even react when I showed up in my gardening overalls.

With this, Claes Manor gained yet another regular visitor, and I gained a great friend.

My name is Sophia Ascart, eldest daughter of the Ascart family. My father is Count Ascart, the King's trusted chancellor. He was a gentle person, just like my mother and brother. I was born into privilege, blessed with a kind and loving family.

I was truly happy… and perhaps that is why it happened, as a price for my blessings.

I was born different than the others around me. My hair was stark white, as if all color had faded from it. My eyes were red as blood.

My appearance was abnormal. People would cast their curious gazes at me, and eventually whisper about me in the shadows, calling me a cursed child.

Even so, my family loved me dearly. My father, who would gently pat my head; my mother, who would lovingly hold me; and my dear brother, who was always at my side, doing everything in his power to protect me.

My gentle family told me that one day, someone who understood me would appear. They told me that I would surely be able to make great friends… but I did not think that was true. That was why I shut myself in my room. I did not want anyone to look upon me, so I isolated myself as much as possible.

In my quiet room, I read book after book. The wondrous, beautiful stories within transported me away from my cruel reality. When I was reading, I could forget about all my troubles.

Amongst these books, my favorite was one about a friendship between a princess and a young commoner girl — *Princess Emerald and Sophia*.

The girl in the story shared my name. But in the story, Sophia was popular and cheerful, with a head full of jet-black hair and sparkling black eyes.

The princess in the story would eventually cross paths with Sophia. *"What beautiful hair you have… Would you mind if I ran my fingers through it, just ever so slightly?"* the princess said, turning to Sophia with a gentle smile. Sophia smiled back shyly.

It was a splendid story… one that a cursed child like me could not possibly experience. This was why I continued locking myself up in my room, fantasizing about becoming Sophia — the Sophia in the stories with Princess Emerald. In my imagination, at least, I could be popular and loved by those around me.

"Sophia, please go to the tea party at the royal castle," my father said to me, gently as ever, one day.

Up until now, I had never attended any sort of tea party. After all… a single step outside was all it took for people to start whispering about my cursed appearance.

So… I really did not want to go outside. I told my gentle father how I felt. I really did not want to go. But my father, who usually gave in to my demands, did not agree that day.

"Listen, Sophia. Magic dwells in you, and when you come of age, you will be enrolled in the academy, just like your peers. It would not do you much good to stay cooped up in your room all day. The upcoming tea party is hosted by the royal princes, and many noble children will be in attendance. Some of them will even attend the academy with you. If it hurts or becomes difficult, Sophia, then you can come home early — but at the very least, you need to see a little more of the outside world."

Of course, I knew this was true. When I reached fifteen years of age, I would be forced to attend the academy. Even I knew that I could not remain in my room forever, lost in my fantasies and stories.

"At the very least, you need to see a little more of the outside world," my father had said. He was right... So regardless of my misgivings, I did my best to muster up some courage, and decided to attend this tea party.

And so, I attended a tea party for the very first time with my brother Nicol. It was a large and fancy party, held in one of the corners of the royal gardens. I had never seen so many people in one place before.

At first I wandered around with my brother, looking at various snacks and teas that I did not recognize. But then we were separated, and I found myself surrounded by a group of other noble children. All of them had the same severe, judgmental expressions. They ended up bringing me to a tree on the outskirts of the tea party, and we all stood under it.

"Do you even know how important of an occasion this is? This is the first tea party hosted by the royal princes!"

"That's right! If a cursed child like you shows up at an event like this, you'll spoil everything!"

"Why are you even here? You shouldn't be showing that shameful face of yours around!"

They surrounded me, all the while saying terrible things. I knew that I looked disgusting... I knew that people hated me. All I could do was stand quietly, biting my lip in silence.

I should never have left my room. I would have been safe if I stayed locked up, and something like this would not happen to me.

Just as those thoughts crossed my mind...

"Do excuse me, but you're in my way."

A clear voice rang out from behind me. I turned around, and standing before me was a girl. She was cool, composed, and elegant... just like Princess Emerald herself. When did she appear? How did she get there...?

With her cool dismissal, the bullies that had surrounded me scattered to the winds. It was all so sudden, and I did not understand what was happening — but I did know that this girl had helped me.

I could only stand in place, stunned, as the girl smiled at me in that same composed and confident manner. Soon she turned around, briskly walking off to some unknown destination.

For a while, my eyes were trained on her silhouette, and all I could do... was stare. I hid behind the tree, afraid that the bullies would return. I only made my way back to the tea party after affirming that they were indeed gone... and as fate would have it, I crossed paths with the girl from earlier.

I should thank her for helping me... And so, I mustered up my courage, approaching her with a shaky voice. "Um..."

She turned around in an impossibly graceful manner, with that same calm and collected expression on her face.

"Um... a-about just now..."

I was too nervous. My voice... it wouldn't come out. Her azure eyes stared straight into mine... then her lips parted, and she spoke.

"What pretty hair you have. Just like strands of silk... Would you mind if I ran my fingers through it, just ever so slightly?"

"...Ah?!"

It was a line from *Princess Emerald and Sophia*... I would know, having read it dozens of times. It was what was said to the bright and cheerful Sophia as she crossed paths with a mysterious girl in town... A girl with an aura of refinement and confidence. Her name was...

"...Princess Emerald," I said, without thinking.

And then…

"Princess Emerald! From the romance novels! M-Maybe! You know of *Princess Emerald and Sophia* too?!"

Before I knew it, the girl had her hands on my shoulders. I could only stand in shocked silence. Why did this girl suddenly say one of Princess Emerald's lines…? Why was she holding me so tightly by the shoulders? I… I did not know what was going on anymore…

The only way people had ever looked at me was either cold or judgmental. And yet… this girl's eyes were sparkling — they shone as she looked straight at me.

I have never seen anyone look at me in this manner before… What is going on?

Caught in the moment, I could only meekly nod as the girl asked me a variety of questions, getting more excited by the minute.

"…What are you doing, Big Sister?"

A surprised voice from the sidelines. I turned, and there stood a handsome youth with brown hair and blue eyes. He was speaking to the girl.

"Wah! I-I apologize." The girl finally let go of me at the boy's question. She then curtsied most elegantly, finally introducing herself. "I do apologize for my manners. I am Katarina Claes. Very pleased to make your acquaintance."

Her mannerisms and countenance… it was really like she was Princess Emerald, in the flesh. I soon realized that I had to return the greeting with one of my own, and quickly did so in a somewhat panicked manner. "…Sophia Ascart."

And then… a most unbelievable thing occurred.

"Lady Sophia! If it would please you, would you like to speak in greater detail with me?"

Katarina's hands were now holding mine. *What is this girl saying...? Does she know who... what, I am?* I could not understand the situation, and only stood still, silent. And then —

"Well then, Lady Sophia. If you would like, please feel free to pay a visit to Claes Manor."

"...Ah... um. Yes. I will."

Before I knew it, I had promised Katarina that I would pay her a visit. Even as we finalized the details of my attendance, I felt lost and confused — no longer sure if this was reality, or the dreams and fantasies that I had always imagined while locked away in my room.

The day of the visit arrived. I had never gone outside on my own, and so naturally, my caring brother accompanied me.

My brother was a year older than me, with a head of raven-black hair and deep, thoughtful eyes. He had come along to protect me, and having him next to me was truly reassuring.

And so I mustered up my courage and made the trip to Claes Manor. When we arrived, the servants who welcomed us stared at me with expressions of surprise and shock. Although I was already used to all this, I could feel what little courage I had gathered rapidly fading.

Perhaps this is all just another prank... As my unease consumed me, she appeared. Her refined features, her rapid breaths — it seemed like she had rushed all the way here. Katarina, however, simply stared at us, not saying a single word.

Is it true? Is it all just a joke, after all? Was I mistaken in coming here? I froze in place, and words never left my lips. My dependable brother, however, spoke up in my stead.

"Thank you very much for extending an invitation to my sister. My sister seldom ventures out on her own, so I have come with her. My name is Nicol. I am Sophia's elder brother."

As if shaken awake by my brother's words, Katarina promptly offered her own response. "No, the pleasure is all mine. Thank you for coming. I am Katarina Claes."

Thank you for coming…? So this isn't some prank or joke? Is it… really alright for me to be here?

"Nicol Ascart, elder brother of Sophia Ascart. Pleased to make your acquaintance," my brother said, once again stating his name.

For some reason, Katarina froze for a moment, not moving in the slightest. *I wonder what's wrong…* I called out to her, worried about her strange state. "…Um. Lady Katarina…?"

"Oh, Lady Sophia. I do apologize. It is so nice to see you again! If you would like, I would like to continue our previous conversation…"

And with that, Katarina invited us to a table seemingly prepared for the occasion, with tea, snacks, and all.

While I felt very uneasy at first, that unpleasant feeling slowly faded as I started speaking with Katarina. It was the first time I had ever been able to speak with someone else about the books I loved. Time passed as if it were a dream.

And just like a dream, it was fleeting — before I knew it, the sun was setting. One of our servants leaned in, informing me that it was time for the dream to end.

I stood up, ready to go, and it was then that Katarina called out to me. "What beautiful hair you have… Would you mind if I ran my fingers through it, just ever so slightly?"

"…Ah?!" I could only stare blankly, my features frozen in confusion. *What is she talking about…? There's no way this disgusting white hair of mine could be beautiful…*

Before I could stop myself, I asked the question I had wanted to ask all this time. It was that nagging suspicion I'd had in my mind ever since I had met her: "…Are you not disgusted by my appearance, Lady Katarina?"

Those looks that were leveled at me as I ventured to the outside world, and the whispers in the shadows, speaking of how repulsive my appearance was…

"…Does it not disgust you, Lady Katarina? This… hair of mine, white as an elderly woman… And these blood-red eyes. Everyone calls me a disgusting, cursed child."

There was not a single part of me that could be beautiful in any way. I was nothing more than a disgusting thing to be avoided, something for others to avert their gazes from. Nothing more…

"…Cursed? What do you mean…?" Katarina said, sounding confused.

"Malicious rumors. From certain individuals who are jealous of our family's achievements. Such jealousy causes them to spread these baseless accusations." My brother's voice echoed coldly through the room. My kind brother, my family — once again protecting me from the world…

"…Even so. It does little to change the fact that my appearance is disgusting and revolting." There was no shortage of heartless statements directed at my strange appearance. It had always been this way. *Why was I born like this…? I wish I had been born beautiful… like Sophia from my favorite story.*

"Well I think you're really pretty." Katarina said.

Pretty? What is she talking about…? I stared straight at her.

"I think your silky white hair is beautiful. I think your ruby-red, sparkling eyes are beautiful. I think… you… are beautiful," Katarina said, smiling at me.

Silky white hair... ruby-red, sparkling eyes. Are these truly words that could be used to describe one such as myself? It's... unbelievable...

Her aqua-blue eyes, however, did not speak of lies as they stared into mine. Katarina... Like a hero of justice, she came to my rescue at the tea party. A girl just like Princess Emerald from my favorite story.

"Actually, I would be so pleased if you would come and visit again! And if you don't mind... would you like to be my friend?" Katarina said, her hands reaching out towards me.

"One day, someone who understands you will appear, Sophia. And you will be great friends." I had never once believed it when any member of my beloved family had told me this. It was, after all, impossible... I'd thought that no one like that could ever exist.

I, who had been treated like an outcast, who was always regarded with strange, fearful gazes. To think that anyone would ask for me to become friends with them...

I slowly took Katarina's hands in my own shivering palms. She held my hands tightly, smiling gently as she held onto them.

Is this a dream...? I could no longer tell as I sat in the carriage, still stunned from the events. My brother, however, smiled at me — a smile that I did not often see. "I am glad that you have made a friend."

A friend... I thought that it would be impossible for a person like me. That was why I had remained holed up in my room, with nothing but my imagination and daydreams for company. In reality... I had wanted, desired, a friend. For the longest time... that was all I ever wanted.

I recalled the warmth of Katarina's hands and the happy smile on her face. I had always wanted someone like that... but then, I had given up. And now, I held that very thing... tight in my hands.

From then on, we continued our visits to Claes Manor, and in doing so got to know some of Katarina's other friends, including her brother and the two princes. Before I knew it, my previously cramped and isolated world had expanded — almost impossibly, in the blink of an eye. Mary, another friend of Katarina's, said this to me:

"A while ago... I hated myself. I hated the red color of my hair and eyes."

I was surprised. Mary was much like Katarina, a noble lady of certain means... and yet, she hated herself...? *Look at her beautiful hair, her stunning eyes!* I couldn't believe what I was hearing.

"But... when Lady Katarina told me that I was charming, that I was cute, and that she liked me for who I was... I found that I could no longer hate myself. I found that I loved my hair, my eyes... And so, Lady Sophia, I think that you will be quite alright as well," Mary said, looking at me earnestly.

None of the people who gathered at this manor, Mary included, thought of me as disgusting. Katarina herself said that my hair and my eyes were beautiful, wonderful things. All the people I had met up until now had hated me, but Katarina was different. Her heartfelt praise made this clear.

Will I one day come to love myself, like Mary has...? Will a day ever come where I will be able to accept this strange appearance of mine?

The future was still a mystery to me. Even so, I now felt that such a day could eventually come to pass.

"Thank you very much," I said gratefully to Mary.

Mary smiled brazenly, much like Katarina. "Just so you know... I have no intention of handing Lady Katarina over."

I once thought that reading alone in my room was the best thing I could ever do. I never knew that I would find something so much more amazing... in this wondrous world that I had suddenly been thrust into.

As summer reached its end, the world was now colored in the beginnings of autumn. Several weeks had passed since Sophia and Nicol first visited me at my house.

With the addition of Sophia, even Mary got interested and joined us in the romance novel boom. Thanks to Sophia's bookworm nature and encyclopedic knowledge, the genres covered in our meetings expanded.

The romance novel I was currently obsessed with was a story about a devilishly dashing count and his romance with a younger girl. The Count was so incredibly breathtaking that he charmed both men and women alike — but he falls in love with a normal girl living in a small town. It was a sweet story of love and romance. Sophia recommended it to me, of course. The Count in the book was an incredibly beautiful young man, with jet-black hair and eyes.

"Actually... I noticed that the Count looked like my brother, and so I ended up liking this series..." Sophia told me in a whisper. "My opinion may be biased... he is my brother, after all..." She seemed embarrassed.

But the more I read the novel, the more I noticed the similarities. Although Jeord, Keith, and Alan were all handsome in different ways, Nicol's charms were something else — his doll-like features and smooth black hair, and eyes that had the mysterious power of drawing people deeper and deeper into his gaze... As he got older and more mature, I could definitely see him becoming like the "alluring count" in the novel, bewitching both men and women alike.

There were still many unknowns when it came to Nicol. From what I'd written in the *Fortune Lover* manual, Nicol had the least deviant personality among the game's potential love interests. He was also the brother of one of my best friends, so I wanted to be friends with him too. But Nicol was a boy of few words. When he did speak, the conversation always ended in one or two sentences.

Since my life was so busy and bustling, the naturally quiet Nicol hardly had a chance to speak with me much, if at all. Even so, his actions showed his love for Sophia, and he even put up with all our antics. He really was a good brother — it was easy to see why Sophia would look up to him. In fact, I'd heard that Nicol excelled in academics and the sword. He was very accomplished, just like Jeord and Alan.

If I get the opportunity, I'd like to get to know him better. Not long after I had this thought, an opportunity appeared.

"If you would like... we could have a reading session at my home..."

I had been pestering Sophia about letting me see her book collection for a while now, so she eventually invited me over. I kind of felt like I'd pushed her into it, but anyway.

"Really?! Can I really come?!" I exclaimed, jumping up and down happily.

Sophia simply smiled at me, while Anne's eyebrows furrowed and twitched. "Madam would be most displeased to see you behave as such, young miss..."

And so, I finally planned a visit to the Ascart family home. Although I was mainly there to go through Sophia's books and talk about novels, I also hoped to talk with Nicol a little more. It was important to get to know him a little better, especially since he and Sophia were so close. I steeled myself, determined to get more than two sentences out of Nicol during my visit.

When the day arrived, I hopped onto the carriage eagerly, excited to get my hands on Sophia's prized collection. Keith was coming with me, apparently because I was too "socially inept" to go alone. Mother was worried as usual, giving me a warning as I left. "Do be careful, Katarina. And please, do not embarrass yourself."

Typical Mother! I had been to many tea parties now and had even visited Mary's manor. Of course there wouldn't be any problems.

When we arrived at the Ascart family home, I found that it wasn't as big as Claes Manor, but it was clean, organized, and decorated nicely. We were led by the servants to a reception area with tea.

Then, just as we were about to settle in, two people entered the room. One was a handsome man, and the other was an elegant and dignified lady. They seemed to be about the same age as my parents. I was expecting my friend Sophia, not this impossibly beautiful couple! I was stunned, staring at them in awe.

Who exactly are these beautiful people? Just as that thought crossed my mind, the man turned to me, smiling brightly.

"A pleasure to meet you. I am Nicol and Sophia's father, Dan Ascart. This is my wife, Radia."

"Radia Ascart. A pleasure."

Having delivered their greetings, they both smiled gently in welcome. *What?! These are Sophia and Nicol's parents?!* That made sense, since they were intimidatingly beautiful.

If this was the case… this must be the rumored royal chancellor, the King's trusted right arm.

I turned to Madam Ascart to see that she was still smiling gently. Like Nicol, Count Ascart had black hair, while his wife had pale, golden-blonde hair and blue eyes. They looked like characters straight out of a fairy tale, just like I would have expected of Nicol and Sophia's parents.

Still stunned by their fairy-tale radiance, I continued staring at them both, mouth agape, until Keith gave my hand a slight push.

"Big Sister… your greetings…" Keith whispered.

That's right! I really should be doing the noble lady greeting thing…

"…The pleasure is mine. I am Katarina Claes. Thank you very much for inviting me here on this day."

"I am her younger brother, Keith Claes. Thank you for having us."

As soon as I had delivered the elegant greeting of a young noble lady, Keith followed up with his own. *There, we did our introductions. But what are Sophia's parents doing here?* They could probably see the confusion on my face.

"We wanted to greet you first," Count Ascart said quickly, answering my unspoken question. "Sophia and her brother have not been informed yet that you have arrived, you see. She is probably fidgeting up there in her room, waiting for you as we speak."

"Is that so…?" That answered why they were here, but this was the first time someone else's parents had come to greet me in person. It made me nervous.

I had visited Mary's home several times, but her father was often busy and out of the house. In fact, I hadn't seen him ever since the very first tea party I'd attended. Visiting a friend's house was nothing new to me, but having their parents show up to greet me was. I was so nervous that I clammed up, standing stiff like a board.

Madam Ascart approached me elegantly. "I have heard many things about you from my daughter, Lady Katarina. Ever since she met you, Sophia has been so happy... Thank you very much," she said, before holding out a hand.

Now that I was looking at her up close, I was struck by her beauty again. She looked a lot like Sophia... or was it the other way around? Reaching out nervously, I took her outstretched hand in mine.

"I am most grateful as well. I greatly enjoy speaking with Lady Sophia. I will be glad if we can continue being friends." I was able to live this new, fulfilling romance novel life mainly because of Sophia. If I hadn't met her, my life wouldn't be enriched by all these wonderful stories. Of course I'd want to continue being friends with her.

Upon hearing my words, Madam Ascart, who really did look like Sophia, squeezed my hand tightly. "I am so, so glad... that Sophia has a wonderful friend like you."

And with that, Madam Ascart and the Count both bowed their heads. "I would like to thank you too. Lady Katarina Claes... thank you. Truly."

"Oh...? Ah, yes, thank you too, yes..." My nervousness peaked as the beautiful couple bowed to me, of all people! I was completely flustered. I wanted to respond by saying something dignified, but I'd totally messed up! Even so, both Count and Madam Ascart just kept smiling at me warmly, ignoring my panic. *What gentle, kind parents!*

And with those same welcoming smiles, they left the room, telling me that they would fetch Sophia. Even the way they left was beautiful. I couldn't help but sigh as my eyes followed them out of the reception room. *...They really made me nervous. But I'm glad that I'm welcome in their household!*

In my experience, it was harder for me to give a good impression than it would be for a normal person. I blamed my villainess face. Any time I tried to smile elegantly, I ended up looking evil instead. In fact, I'm sure that was what happened at the royal tea party when those children all scattered after I came down from the tree. One was all it took! What a sad memory.

Once the Ascart couple were out of earshot, I leaned in and whispered to Keith. "What beautiful, kind parents Sophia has!"

"I agree, Big Sister," Keith said with a smile.

"If only Mother was like Madam Ascart! I wish she was a little calmer. All that frowning and getting mad is going to give her wrinkles."

"I, too, think that Mother would very much like to live peacefully..." Keith said, looking at me with a strangely sad expression as I complained about how our mother wasn't at all like the kind and beautiful Madam Ascart.

What does he mean by that? I stared at Keith with blank eyes, but my brother just sighed.

That was when Sophia entered the room. Following close behind her was Nicol, as usual. Sophia seemed to be breathing irregularly and her cheeks were a little flushed. Nicol, on the other hand, didn't seem winded at all even though he probably traveled at the same speed.

"Welcome, Lady Katarina!" Sophia said, smiling slightly with her cheeks red. *Cute as always!*

I had a lot of fun talking with Sophia, and also looking through the Ascart family's study with its amazing collection of books. That was where Sophia kept her personal collection, and I was delighted as I went through them. Things were different than usual though, because Keith was there to keep Nicol company. Now that he had a boy his age around, even the infamously silent Nicol had some things to say. While the boys weren't as loud as me and Sophia, I noticed that they were talking whenever I glanced over at them.

Time flies when you're having fun. Even though my tutoring and etiquette lessons felt like they took forever, the time I spent with Sophia seemed to pass in seconds. I wanted to stay longer, but Mother would be angry since she'd told me not to inconvenience my hosts.

Hugging books that I was borrowing from Sophia close to my chest, I packed up and got ready for the trip home with Keith. Just as we were about to say goodbye to the Ascart siblings...

"Oh no! I left behind the book I'd recommended to you, Katarina..." Sophia exclaimed, looking surprisingly shocked.

"Oh yeah, that book we were talking about, right?" It was the top book on Sophia's recommendations list. She was telling me about it passionately in the study, and had forgotten to take the book with her when she came to see us off.

"Yes, that book. I apologize... I will go fetch it right away."

"That's okay, Sophia! Maybe I can borrow it next time?"

Sophia seemed ready to dash off. "No, it really is an amazing book... I do hope that you can read it as soon as possible...! Please, it will just be a moment." She ran off in the direction of the study. Well, noble ladies in dresses didn't really run, but she did rush as much as she could.

Seeing Sophia take off like that reminded me of a friend in my previous life, Acchan. If Sophia had known me back then, we would have read manga, watched anime, and maybe even played otome games together. *I'm so lucky to have such great friends!*

As I watched Sophia go, the normally silent Nicol suddenly turned to me. "Lady Katarina Claes. Allow me to thank you for being friends with Sophia. I am grateful from the bottom of my heart."

Oh yeah, I did want to talk to Nicol today... I had forgotten about my plan when I'd gotten lost in the books and novels with Sophia in the study. *Now is my chance!* Now I'd be able to talk to him more.

"No, the pleasure is all mine. In fact, I am grateful that Lady Sophia is friends with someone like me. Actually, your parents said the same thing to me earlier..."

"My... parents?"

I realized I had forgotten to tell Nicol and Sophia about our short meeting with their parents. "Yes, they took the trouble to personally show up at the reception room before your arrival. They are truly wonderful parents."

"...Is that so? Thank you, Lady Katarina," Nicol said expressionlessly. And with that, the conversation was over.

While this was the longest conversation I'd ever had with Nicol Ascart, it hardly counted as a conversation! How did Keith get him to talk so much?

I wish I had a little of Keith's talent. Or is it because they're both boys? Anyway, I have to try to revive this conversation...

I need a topic... Yes, I know! I can use my knowledge of my past life! I'll show him all of my seventeen years of wisdom! I want to do something better than Keith, for once.

Something... something to continue the conversation. I racked my mind and plumbed my memories. And then... *Oh wait. What about that granny next door who'd talk to me for thirty minutes or more whenever she caught me?*

That's it! That's the thing! That neighbor of mine was a conversational expert, with the power to lengthen even the shallowest conversations. I have to channel her power...!

Yes, I remember her always saying something like this...

"You really are blessed, Master Nicol, to have such amazing parents, and a cute younger sister." I followed up with a full-faced smile, just like that old lady always did. I was inspired by what she'd always tell my dad: that he was a lucky man, having married such a beautiful bride. As soon as she said it, my dad would be as good as gone for the next half an hour.

That talkative granny would be proud of me! However...

"...Blessed...?" For some reason, Nicol's demeanor suddenly changed completely.

"Ah, um..."

"...Do you truly think... that I am blessed?"

Although Nicol's face was still as expressionless as ever, something about it was different. This sudden change left me confused, even scared. *I've really done it now, haven't I?* I must have said it wrong, somehow.

"I do think that you have a wonderful family... um. Was I... mistaken in any way?" I stuttered slowly.

Nicol stared at me, and I felt his black eyes piercing into my soul. And then...

"...No. No, Lady Katarina. You are not mistaken at all. I have two respectable, wonderful parents, and a gentle, cute younger sister. Yes, I am truly blessed," Nicol said, as if pleased. Then... he smiled.

I had known Nicol for a few weeks now, but never once had I seen him smile. I had heard from Sophia that her brother almost never did. But now he was smiling, as if he were really happy. He was always beautiful, but that heartfelt smile seemed to amplify that beauty ten times over.

It was as if the Alluring Count himself — that one from the novel I liked — had appeared before me, bewitching smile and all. It turned out that Nicol was the real Alluring Count this whole time…!

Predictably, I clammed up and froze. It was Sophia's return that freed me from the Count's curse, hugging the book she'd retrieved like it was a treasure. "Lady Katarina… here. This book!"

I had finally broken free of the Count's spell thanks to the cute book-hugging Sophia. Turning my head slightly, I saw Keith, who was also rooted to the spot. Nicol, on the other hand, had gone back to his usual emotionless self.

This is bad! My innocent brother has been charmed by the Alluring Count's power! I don't want Keith to fall in love with the protagonist, but that doesn't mean I wanted him to fall for another boy! If this goes on, my treasured brother might get into trouble!

After gratefully accepting the book from Sophia, I strategically put myself between Keith and Nicol all the way to the carriage. We waved our goodbyes and boarded, and soon left the Ascart family home behind. On the way back…

"Nicol was really the Alluring Count all this time… will I be able to protect Keith from his clutches…?"

"…To think that yet another rival would surface… Just how many temptations must she be showered with…?"

Both Keith and I each stared out of our windows, muttering to ourselves quietly.

I am the eldest son of Count Ascart's family — Nicol Ascart. My father took me to the castle many times in my youth, owing to the fact that he was the royal chancellor. As a result, I had many opportunities to mingle with the princes of this kingdom, especially the two twin princes, who were a year younger than me.

It was about a year ago when these two princes, whom I had known from childhood, began to change. The incessantly perfect Jeord, the third prince, always had a fake smile on his face. His eyes only spoke of boredom; nothing was reflected in them. One day, however, he said that he had "found something most interesting"... and then, he smiled. Yet it was quite dissimilar to his regular expression. With time, Jeord began to change. His false smile disappeared, and in its place was a sparkling vigor.

Jeord's brother, Alan, was the fourth prince. Alan often compared himself to Jeord and pushed him away at every turn. His desperation seemed to only bring him pain. Even Alan, however, started to change with time. As if a great weight had been lifted off his shoulders, Alan stopped resisting Jeord. Instead, he started putting effort into furthering his musical talents — which was where his interests originally lay. His talent was formidable, and almost overnight, people were lauding him as a prodigy of music.

However, the most marked change of all was the fact that Alan would now speak normally with Jeord, whom he used to despise. Those in the castle were surprised, bewildered even, by this. They found it strange that Alan's attitude towards Jeord, which had always been one of defiance and resistance, would change.

In fact, the changes went beyond the two just speaking normally with each other. They started leaving the castle grounds together, and as of late, they had even been seen speaking cordially within the castle grounds. A truly theatrical change.

The reason for this profound change remained a mystery to most, however. The rumors, when they eventually came, spoke of a place they were known to frequent — Claes Manor, home to Duke

Claes and his family. Something or someone within that manor was the reason why such a change had come over the two princes...

On a day not long after the tea party at the royal castle, we made our way to the notorious Claes Manor. My sister, who had attended the party with me, had apparently received a formal invitation from the eldest daughter of the Claes family, Lady Katarina Claes.

My sister, Sophia Ascart, is a gentle and lovable girl. A noble lady of good standing in her own right. Sophia does stand out, however, with her porcelain-white hair and red eyes.

And because of this, because Sophia was a little different, she was exposed to the cruel whims of society. They would look upon her strangely as she walked, and those jealous of our family's achievements claimed that she was a "cursed child."

Even more cruel were the foolish children who took those words literally. With their heartless gazes and words, these people would hurt Sophia. She eventually cooped herself up in her room, no longer willing to face the world. For a few years, Sophia remained that way — closed to the outside world...

Until the day when those two princes held a tea party at the royal castle, which we both attended. Sophia did not seem too enthusiastic about going, and neither was I.

The two princes had met with Sophia several times before. I knew that they would not cast discriminatory looks upon her, nor consider themselves above her. The party, however, was large in scale — as expected of one held by the twin princes.

The children, young lords and ladies of many noble families, would also be in attendance. There would surely be some amongst them who would shun and bemoan Sophia's presence, thinking themselves superior. I did not wish for Sophia to go to such a place, but my father convinced us otherwise.

"Both you and Sophia have magic within. At the age of fifteen, you will both have to attend the Academy of Magic. Remember that you and Sophia are different in both gender and age, so you will not always be able to protect her as you do now. Sophia has to learn how to protect herself. With that many children gathered, I am sure that she will even make some friends."

We, the Ascart siblings, did have magic in our veins. All children like us must enroll at the academy once they come of age, according to the laws of the land. I would do so in four years, with Sophia following suit a year after me.

I wanted to stay by her side as long as possible. I wanted to protect my precious sister. However, given our differences in age and gender, there was no way I could watch over her forever.

Before Sophia had shut herself in, my parents had attempted to take her out to similar outings in the past to make friends, so they said. Children, however, are exceptionally sensitive to those who were... different, from themselves. In the end, those efforts only ended up hurting Sophia.

I understood that this could not possibly go on. However... the prospect of seeing Sophia cry once more was infinitely more terrifying to me.

At the tea party, despite my efforts, I was separated from my sister. I was truly pathetic. How could I think of protecting Sophia like this? Many of those terrible noble children, the very same ones that had hurt her before, were also present at this party. Surely they would hurt her again, now that I was separated from her. There was no doubt about it. With this thought in mind, I could hardly calm myself.

And so I desperately searched for my sister, but to no avail. It was only at the end of the party that I had finally found her. Sophia, however, was simply standing still with a blank expression on her face.

"What have they done to you? Who was it?" I asked, worried.

"Someone by the name of Lady Katarina Claes... has invited me to visit her manor," Sophia muttered with the same blank expression.

And so the two of us headed to Claes Manor. Honestly speaking, I wasn't too enthusiastic about this turn of events — if only because Sophia had received many similar invitations before... only for them to spurn her and turn her away at the gates.

Worry clouded my mind. I had little choice but to approach Jeord, Katarina's fiancé, about Katarina herself. I referred to how she had been kind to Sophia at the party and had invited my sister to her manor.

"There she goes after another noble young lady... And to think I believed she had learned some restraint..."

"Hm...?"

Jeord muttered to himself for a while, before finally looking up at me with a knowing smile. "Nicol, I will admit, Katarina is... strange. She would not, however, hurt your most beloved sister."

Trusting in Jeord's words, but yet still concerned for Sophia, I ended up following her to the Claes family manor.

"I think your silky white hair is beautiful. I think your ruby-red, sparkling eyes are beautiful. I think... you... are beautiful," Katarina Claes said, smiling at Sophia. "Actually, I would be so pleased if you would come and visit again! And if you don't mind... would you like to be my friend?"

Those were the girl's words. She was gently smiling as she held Sophia's hands in hers. As Jeord said, there was no way she would hurt my precious sister.

As I stared at Katarina's gentle smile, I finally realized that she was the one. She was the reason why those changes had come over Jeord and Alan. She was a most mysterious girl, with a unique aura. The twin princes visited this manor simply to spend time with her.

Just like those before her, Sophia changed after meeting Katarina Claes. Before, she had never wanted to take a single step outside her room. Now she clamored to be let out every single day. A light from within had brightened her pained, dark features as a smile returned to her face. I was deeply, deeply grateful towards Katarina Claes.

With Sophia's increasing number of outings, however, came the whispered rumors and insults in the shadows. However, I had no intention of standing by and seeing my now-smiling sister return to her dark, lonely room. So I applied the appropriate kinds of pressure on those who would dare speak ill of Sophia. I silenced the voices in the shadows. I suppose I had not been forceful enough before, but now I renewed my efforts. And with that, the whispers eventually faded.

Even so, as the gossip-mongers eventually disappeared...

"Master Nicol is most unfortunate, having to do all that just for that sister of his!"

"Master Nicol is most capable... but those rumors! All because of his sister! What a pity..."

"How very unfortunate for the Ascarts... to have people talk behind their back because of that child."

The condemnations, gossip, and disdain, had all but ceased, but in their place was pity. Empathy, perhaps? The harder I worked to protect Sophia, the louder the voices became. They were not hostile by any means; they merely pitied me, apparently, for having to do all this. They spoke of how unfortunate I was.

However... those words pierced my heart mercilessly. I was not some victim to be pitied. My family was in no way unfortunate. I had two respectable parents, and a lovely sister. They were family I could be proud of. If anything, I thought that I was fortunate. But no one around me understood this. If I claimed to be happy, they would assume that I was merely putting up with it.

This infuriated me. I was blessed, and yet they decided that I was unfortunate and worthy of pity. *Don't you dare think of my precious sister as a source of misfortune! I've been nothing but happy ever since Sophia was born...!*

I grew tired of this unsolicited pity, but I thought that it was no longer important, even if no one ever understood. My precious sister was now smiling and laughing. And that, to me... was everything. Even if bystanders thought of me as an unfortunate victim... even if they would never understand, it would be just fine.

"You really are blessed, Master Nicol, to have such amazing parents, and a cute younger sister." Katarina Claes, the girl in front of me, spoke with that same gentle smile on her face. It was that exact smile that she had shown to Sophia, one that gave off a gentle, warm light.

"...Blessed...?"

Yes. Exactly as I had always thought. But... no one would understand me. No one sought to.

"Ah, um…"

"…Do you truly think… that I am blessed?" I said, staring straight at Katarina.

"I do think that you have a wonderful family… um. Was I… mistaken in any way?" Katarina stared back, her aqua-blue eyes looking into mine.

"…No. No, Lady Katarina. You are not mistaken at all. I have two respectable, wonderful parents, and a gentle, cute younger sister. Yes, I am truly blessed."

I had thought that no one would ever understand. I had already given up. And yet this girl, Katarina, understood. I had assumed that I was alone, and that no one would ever feel the same way that I did, but I was wrong. The indignation in my heart slowly started to fade as I gazed upon the girl standing before me.

The eldest daughter of Duke Claes, Katarina Claes. The mysterious girl who has changed those twin princes and the first to understand these thoughts of mine, when I had already long given up on empathy and understanding.

I finally understood why the princes and my sister were so eager to visit Claes Manor. Again and again, day after day. I suppose it is reasonable to assume that I shall soon take after them. Not just to escort Sophia and to keep her safe — but to spend time with Katarina Claes.

Time flew by quickly. I could remember everything that happened that spring when I was eight years old as if it were yesterday, but before I knew it, seven years had passed.

I was fifteen, meaning that I was now of age and expected to debut in society as a noble young lady. And of course, following the law, I would be attending the Academy of Magic with all the other magically gifted teens.

I turned fifteen this summer, so I would be going to the academy in the spring of next year. It was a boarding school, and all students had to stay in the dormitories regardless of social standing. Although the teens from elite families were given their own private rooms and took servants with them, we noble children would have much less freedom than we were used to.

Upon entering the academy... the terrifying otome game would begin. The protagonist, a commoner who was born with the rare power of Light Magic, would come to the Academy of Magic and all its noble teens. She would then attract the attention of the twin princes, the son of a duke, and the son of a chancellor. Those incredibly handsome and popular boys would all fall for her.

Meanwhile, the villainess Katarina Claes, the antagonist in some of these scenarios, would head towards a Catastrophic Bad End.

As I thought back on these past seven years, I reassured myself that I had put all my effort into avoiding these bad endings. I'd used many strategies: improving my skill with the sword, practicing the applications of my magic, making sure Keith was never lonely, and improving my projectile snake creation.

I did have some successes. I was told that my swordplay had improved a lot, Keith wasn't withdrawn at all anymore, and my toy snakes were more lifelike with each new prototype. But there was one thing that didn't go so well: strengthening my magic.

Since the beginning, I was never any good at magic. Although I did increase the size of my Dirt Bump from two to fifteen centimeters within a year, that was as far as it went. No matter how much I trained, the lump of earth never got any taller, and I could never use any other kind of magic.

I was in denial about this at first, but eventually I realized that I just had to accept it. I wasn't happy about it, but nothing could change the fact that I was just naturally bad at magic. I was told that the lessons at the academy were supposed to awaken my hidden potential, but I didn't have high hopes.

And so, my original plan of using my apparently "rare" magical powers to find a job if I were exiled from the kingdom had to be scrapped. There was no way it would work out. So how could I keep myself afloat?

While I was thinking about that very question, one of my servants mentioned something interesting to me. "It is common practice for large farming families to employ other farmers to work their fields and whatnot."

That's it! My agricultural skills had improved over the years, and my plants didn't wither anymore. I think I was pretty darn good at fieldwork now. If I got exiled, I could look for a large farming family and get hired as a farm hand. As long as I could find work, I'd be okay.

So I continued my magical training, though I put more of my effort into my agricultural studies instead, just in case I'd really have to turn farming into a livelihood.

With that, my contingency plans were complete. I soldiered on, honing my skills and improving my strategies. But there was one thing that I didn't account for in my plans: the fact that all the romantic interests of *Fortune Lover* had ended up gathering at my house on a regular basis, and that I now had different relationships with all of them.

First, there was Jeord Stuart. The third prince of the kingdom, and the fiancé of Katarina Claes. Although he appeared to be a fairy-tale prince with his blonde hair and blue eyes, he was actually a terrible, twisted sadist. If Jeord fell for the protagonist, Katarina would be headed for a Catastrophic Bad End without a doubt.

While Jeord was completely uninterested in Katarina and hardly had any contact with her within the setting of *Fortune Lover*, before I knew it, he was visiting my manor every few days. I often gave him vegetables and fruits from my harvest, and he would send snacks and candies my way as thanks. It seemed that we were friends; after all, we spent lots of time together.

Weirdly, I got along really well with Jeord. It was hard for me to imagine that he would suddenly come at me with his sword or exile me from the kingdom. But I knew that if he met the protagonist and fell for her, I would be in the way. According to a novel I read recently, *"Love can change a person."* I couldn't let my guard down.

Actually, the scar on my forehead that led to this entire engagement in the first place had vanished a while ago. Once I noticed this, I immediately sent for Jeord, eager to tell him about it.

"Prince Jeord, the scar on my forehead has completely vanished. As such, you no longer need to take responsibility for me. I wouldn't mind if the engagement were canceled," I said, happy to inform Jeord of his freedom.

Jeord seemed surprised. His eyes widened for a moment, but then he smiled his usual smile. "Is that so? Well then, if you would please show me." He approached me with that ever-smiling face of his and forcefully brushed my bangs aside to inspect my forehead.

As he could plainly see, the scar was completely gone. Or so I thought…

"No, Katarina. There is still quite the scar, from what I can see," Jeord said as he continued to stare at my healed skin.

"Wha? But I've checked many times in the mirror… Anne helped, too…" I muttered, stunned.

"I would suppose you were both mistaken. A scar yet remains here. Do you not think so too?" Jeord said, turning to Anne. As my personal maid, she had been standing next to me all this time.

Although Anne had just agreed with me that the scar was completely a moment ago… she now nodded in agreement. *Et tu, Anne?*

And so the vanished scar on my forehead was declared to still exist. Jeord, still smiling, ended the discussion with a single statement. "So you see, there will be no cancellations with regards to our engagement."

By the way, Mother, who had agreed to the engagement in the beginning, had completely changed her mind. Both she and Keith seemed to believe that "Katarina could not possibly fulfill the duties expected of a queen." But regardless of their protests, my engagement remained unbroken.

As expected of Jeord — this was exactly how things went in *Fortune Lover*. The prince didn't want to let go of his fiancée just yet, probably because she was a convenient barrier against the suitors he'd have to face otherwise.

It was now clear that I wouldn't be able to completely avoid the Catastrophic Bad End that involved being engaged to Jeord. So I decided to bring a sword with me to the academy, along with my best snake toy, the most lifelike so far. I still had more work to do with that, starting with practicing how to pull it out of my pocket as smoothly as possible.

And then there was Keith Claes. My cute adopted brother, who had been brought into the family seven years ago for his impressive magical ability — and a potential love interest. If Keith fell in love with the protagonist, it would all be over for Katarina. A straight line to yet another Catastrophic Bad End.

In the setting of *Fortune Lover*, Keith, with his flaxen hair and green eyes, was ostracized and alienated by his adoptive mother and sister. He ended up becoming a playboy in rebellion against his harsh upbringing. And then he would meet the protagonist at the academy, and would be slowly healed by her love, which wouldn't end well for me. So I worked hard every day to make sure that Keith never felt lonely. He never became a shut-in, and was instead always by my side.

Since Keith wasn't lonely anymore, he probably wouldn't fall for the protagonist. But there was one problem with my plan: To prevent him from becoming a playboy, I constantly told Keith to be respectful and kind to women. The result was... not what I expected.

Keith had become a gentlemanly womanizer, for the lack of a better term. He did as his adoptive sister preached — he was gentle and kind to women, which was great! But as the years passed by and he grew up, he turned from the cute little kid I knew to a young man who caught the eye of all kinds of ladies.

Of course, I hardly noticed this while it was happening. Maybe it was because I spent so much time with Keith, or maybe I just didn't pay attention enough to be affected by his charms. But whatever the reason, it was far too late when I realized that Keith had become so charming and attractive that noble ladies were falling head over heels for him. Even the servants were affected by Keith Claes the ladies' man. While I had stopped Keith from becoming a shut-in, I ended up turning him into a gentlemanly lady-killer instead...

Anyway. Alan Stuart, the fourth prince, Jeord's twin brother, and yet another potential love interest. With his wild looks, silver hair and blue eyes, Alan grew up constantly comparing himself to Jeord and nursing a huge inferiority complex that made him hate his brother. At least, that was how it was in the original setting of *Fortune Lover*.

Alan had instead become a very different person, no longer feeling inferior to Jeord, nor hating him. In fact, while the two weren't exactly the best of friends, they did at least have a functional, cordial relationship.

Katarina Claes never appeared as an antagonist in Alan's route, and originally the two never should have even met. But for one reason or another, Alan ended up visiting me often. Now, having fully embraced his musical talent, he sent me invitations to his piano and violin performances, which I'd attend with Mary and the rest. We were good friends now.

This was strange — in the setting of *Fortune Lover*, Alan never explored his talents like this. In fact, he only started doing so after meeting the protagonist. I couldn't help but notice that this series of events was very different from the plot I remembered.

And then there was Mary Hunt, Alan's fiancée and the rival character of the Alan route. Her eyes and hair were a shade of burnt sienna, perfectly complimenting her features. She was a beautiful, doll-like girl. In the original setting of *Fortune Lover*, Mary hardly had any contact with Katarina Claes, much like Alan.

But now Mary had become one of my closest friends. Even though she was reserved and fearful when I first met her, she changed a lot over the last seven years. She excelled in her studies, and presented herself as an elegant and refined young lady at her social debut not long ago. Apparently people everywhere were talking about her alluring dance steps. She was the perfect example of what a noble lady should be.

According to the original setting, Mary was supposed to be deeply in love with Alan. But the Mary I knew didn't seem to think much of him. They got along just fine, but she never talked about him while we were together, and they didn't seem to ever see each other outside of my manor. Was she just hiding her feelings because she's shy?

Mary was supposed to be the image of a perfect noble lady who also had ambitions to become queen — at least, according to what I remembered from *Fortune Lover*. But now, she didn't seem to have any interest in becoming royalty. In fact, she started saying a few years ago that she was "not at all suited to such an important role as queen." She also told me all the time about how hard it was to live as royalty, and how busy their lives were.

The more I heard from Mary, the more I felt a sense of dread about my apparently inevitable engagement to Prince Jeord. If the idea was daunting to Mary, who was perfect in so many ways, there was no way I could take on the role.

Seeing that I was having doubts about my future, Mary offered a suggestion. "Well then, perhaps we could both break our engagements... and the two of us could escape to some faraway land." *She's such a gentle and reliable friend!*

Next was Nicol Ascart. The silent, ever-expressionless son of Chancellor Ascart... who was, of course, also a potential love interest. A ravishing youth of raven-black hair and eyes; devilishly alluring, capable of charming both man and woman alike with his unique aura. In the game, he had nothing at all to do with Katarina Claes. But I did end up becoming friends with Nicol's younger sister, and so he ended up coming to my manor too.

Nicol only spoke when he had to, remaining stoic and reserved most of the time. But his superhuman charm only increased as the years went by. He smiled more than he used to, probably because he was more comfortable with us now. It really was so charming... *No, no. I will not be swayed. That smile is dangerous!*

He was dangerously attractive, so much so that he was popular not only with the ladies, but with men too. At least, that's what the rumors said. All it took was a glimpse at his beautiful face and faint smile, and anyone would be bewitched.

Nicol had many victims at Claes Manor, as his charm had already put a number of servants under his spell. Even so, I took comfort in the fact that I had somehow managed to protect Keith and Mary from his seductive wiles.

Last but not least, Sophia Ascart. Nicol's younger sister, and the rival character in Nicol's route. Sophia, who was beautiful like her brother, never should have met Katarina Claes either. But now she was a close friend of mine, like Mary, and also my comrade in my obsession with romance novels.

Due to the fact that she had been cooped up in her room until she was about ten, Sophia was a voracious reader, and her recommendations were always good reads. She had the amazing ability to pluck out great pieces from the literary sea. I admired her as the true master in romance novel appreciation.

The amazing Sophia seemed to respect her brother more than anyone else, and talked about him often. "My brother is truly an amazing individual… he would make the ideal husband, if I may say so…" She loved him so much that it was almost like she had a crush on him! At this rate, she'd be really sad if Nicol found someone he likes. If that time ever came, I would comfort her as well as I could!

And so it came to be that I, for some strange reason, became friends with these potential love interests and rival characters, and would soon be starting my academy life with them this spring.

The day of my fifteenth birthday arrived. My social debut party was held at Claes Manor, and had been planned for the past few years.

Not only would I have to greet each and every guest that came through the gates, but I also had to dance. I'm good with physical movement and exercise, but unfortunately, I have no sense of rhythm. I've always struggled with dancing, so I had to endure a hellish training regimen under the watchful eye of my mother so that I'd be able to dance at the party. At least my movements now looked like some kind of dance, but I was still really nervous that I'd slip up.

To make things worse, my escort for the part was Jeord. Apparently it was inappropriate to have anyone but my fiancé escort me, but I wished Keith could do it instead. My brother would simply smile and forgive me if I stepped on his toes, but I didn't expect the same kind of mercy from Jeord.

The more I thought about it, the more gloomy I felt. I was starting to really dread this party. On the day of the event, I felt nervous from the moment I woke up even though the party wasn't until that evening.

By the time my makeup and outfit was double and triple checked and the party was about to start, I was exhausted by worry. A glance in the mirror did show a well-dressed and made-up young lady, thanks for the hard work of my servants. But they couldn't do anything to change the villainous look of my face.

And so I made my way to the venue with Jeord, all dressed up in formal attire and not looking at all like my usual self. After issuing the customary greetings to the guests, he led me to the ballroom so we could start things off with the first dance. I danced carefully, focusing hard so that I wouldn't make any blunders like stepping on his feet.

"You look stunning tonight, Katarina."

"Thank you very much."

I couldn't help but notice the smitten gazes of the other women around me as the blonde haired, blue-eyed prince delivered his lines. Regardless of how Jeord was on the inside, there was no denying that he seemed like an angel from an outside point of view. But as a result, I could feel their jealousy being directed at me, his fiancée. *If they're that envious, I'd happily swap places with them,* I thought as I continued the dance.

"Katarina. Although I may have said this before, do allow me to say this once more; I have absolutely no intention of canceling my engagement with you," Jeord said, smiling.

Jeord said this as we were on the dance floor, even as countless passionate gazes were being directed at him. But of course he would; if he canceled the engagement now, all hell would break loose. He needed someone like me to ward off his endless wave of lady suitors. So...

"...I understand," I said simply.

"I see. So you finally understand, Katarina?"

"Yes… but… um. If you ever do find someone else you like, Prince Jeord, please tell me right away. I will withdraw from the engagement immediately!"

Yes, I would never interfere! In fact, I would pray for Prince Jeord's future happiness! I thought desperately. I had to make sure that I wouldn't become an obstacle that had to be erased!

"…Hmm. I see, Katarina. It would appear that you do not understand at all," Jeord said, his smile twitching slightly.

Wha? Does he not believe me? Even after my passionate declaration?

"Yes, I really do wonder. How exactly should I communicate this to you? Perhaps it was a little early, after all, for the party involved in formulating this… prearranged agreement."

"Hm?" *What's he talking about now?* I had absolutely no idea. *Prearranged agreement? What is that?* Confusion clouded my mind.

"Wah!" Suddenly my sense of balance vanished as I felt something sweep me off my feet. Before I knew what was happening, Jeord was holding me in his arms.

"Um… Erm, Prince Jeord. My apologies." *I got too distracted during the dance!* Since I was so bad at it, I assumed that I'd failed to keep up and had fallen over, forcing Jeord to catch me. I apologized and quickly tried to stand so that Jeord wouldn't have to hold me up.

Hmm? Jeord was holding me tightly, and I couldn't break free. "Um? Prince Jeord…?" In fact, he had me in what could only be described as a tight embrace. *Oh no…! Did I step on his toes when I fell? Is that why he's frozen like this, unable to move?! This is bad! And after I'd tried so hard to be careful…!*

"Prince Jeord… are you alright?" I asked somewhat timidly. But then I realized that the prince was chuckling to himself.

"Ah, but you are really so defenseless, Katarina. If you remain this way, I could simply catch you... anytime," Jeord whispered right next to my ear.

Huh? So I didn't accidentally step on his toes and make him freeze with pain? As I got more confused by the moment, I noticed Jeord's head slowly moving down to my neck — and then I felt a strange sensation on my skin. Before I knew it, I had been released from Jeord's vice-like grip.

"This will do for today, Katarina. But one day... I shall take it all." Jeord's grin made him look like a mischievous child.

So... what was that all about? I was completely baffled. But at least I'd managed to avoid stepping on anyone's toes for now, so that was good.

Eventually, I finished my strange dance with Jeord. Immediately after, Keith walked towards me briskly with a tense expression on his face.

"If you would, Big Sister..." Keith said, withdrawing a handkerchief from his pocket, before placing it on my neck and rubbing it.

"Huh? Hey, Keith, what are you..." *Why is my brother suddenly wiping my neck? I went through a total makeover today, so my neck should be clean...*

"Ah, a small bug landed on your neck, and I was just... cleaning that up for you."

"Oh, really? Thank you, Keith." *A bug, huh? Well, it is summer.* Come to think of it, that strange sensation I had felt on my neck while in Jeord's embrace may have been some sort of bug.

What a bummer for our servants to spend so much time powdering me up and making me look perfect, only for a bug to come along and ruin everything! It was a good thing Keith had noticed it and helped me clean it up.

After finishing his wiping of my neck, Keith turned to me, asking me for a dance. "You look so beautiful, Big Sister."

"Thank you, Keith."

While my brother spoke with his usual, gentle smile, I could feel the many feminine gazes lock onto us. That was natural, since Keith was the heir of the Claes family, and wasn't engaged to anyone yet. There were a lot of noble ladies after him, and his apparently irresistible charm (which I didn't really understand) made him even more attractive to them.

Come to think of it, Keith didn't seem to have anyone he liked, despite being so incredibly popular. In fact, we'd never talked about it together. *I hope Keith gets engaged to an amazing lady — just not the protagonist girl,* I thought as Keith led me along. He really was good at dancing.

But then, the faintly smiling Keith suddenly looked serious. "You know, Big Sister... You really should be a little more aware of the dangers that surround you."

"...Hmm? Aware of... dangers?"

"Yes. Especially when it comes to Prince Jeord."

Ah, he wants his sister to be careful. But why would he mention Jeord? I was already plenty aware of Jeord, cautious even.

"Don't worry! I'm all about sensing danger when it comes to Prince Jeord!"

"...Really, Big Sister? To be honest, it doesn't quite come across that way..." Keith replied, seeming incredulous at my proud response.

"Yes, things are perfect! I am absolutely prepared to call off the whole engagement at any time! I even told him just now that I would, and that I would never get in the way of his true love... I told him!"

"...How is that... perfect, Big Sister? No... this will not do at all. Did you not see what happened just now? How could you be... saying...?" Keith's expression became even more intense as he started muttering rapidly to himself.

Hmm? Did I not do enough? Then... "I could even prepare documents, you know? To call off the engagement. And then all I'd have to do is show them to Prince Jeord..."

"No! No, you mustn't! If you provoke him any further... there may be no telling what he would do..."

What's that supposed to mean? But despite my confusion, Keith kept on trying to warn me against being alone with Jeord. Of course, he had a point. He might exile me if we end up in private, and then I'd be in a lot of trouble. But the protagonist hadn't showed up yet, so I thought I was doing okay so far?

I eventually finished my dance with Keith, who was now wearing a very strange expression and still muttering to himself. Next was apparently Alan, who had just finished his dance with Mary.

Alan casually stuck out his hand in my general direction. "Looking less shabby today, huh?" he said.

Is that even a compliment? I guess I should thank him anyway. "...Thank you very much."

Alan, of course, attracted many passionate gazes from the women on the dance floor — just like Jeord and Keith before him. From what I'd heard, the youthful music prodigy was supposedly sponsored by many older lady patrons. These women would say things like… *"Oh, but that change in personality when he's performing… I can't get enough of it!"* As usual, things like that were beyond me.

Alan's fiancée was Mary, an upstanding noble lady who was well-known and respected. Apparently even Alan's fans wished them well, which meant they were doing pretty well as a couple, unlike me and Jeord. People always said we were *"nothing alike, except in social standing."*

While Alan was a lot more brusque in how he was leading the dance compared to Jeord and Keith, as a musical genius, his rhythm was impeccable. His elegant movements contrasted starkly with his regular attitude. He now seemed more like an adult than ever.

Is this the difference the older ladies were talking about? Maybe not, I dunno. This is too complicated for me to understand. Maybe I'll get it when I'm older.

Well, I'm actually seventeen in my mind. And in demeanor that the older ladies were speaking of? Hmm. Probably not quite… This was all a bit much for me to understand. Maybe I will when I get a bit older?

Well, technically I'm seventeen plus fifteen years of age now, so shouldn't I be adult enough?

…Maybe it's just my body limiting my consciousness! Yes, it has to be that! It's definitely not that I'm a hopeless child who'll never mature. Yep, that's what I choose to believe, I thought to myself encouragingly.

"Hey, you… what's with this spot on your neck?" Alan asked, apparently noticing something.

"On my neck?"

"On the side, right here. It's a little red."

"Oh, that. Well, I was bitten by a bug just now, unfortunately…"

"A bug? A bug indoors?"

"Yes, it isn't a sealed space after all, right? It must have crawled in from somewhere."

"...Really?"

Is this bug bite really that eye-catching? I'd have to make sure to apply some kind of bug spray next time I went to a ball. Actually, did this world even have anything like that?

"Anyway... you really do look different than usual..." Alan said as he took a good look at me.

"Yes, my family's servants spent the entire day doing me up and tidying my hair... and all that." Even I could tell that they did an amazing job when I looked into the mirror. "They did quite a lot. Scrubbed me all over, fixed my dress countless times, and my underwear—"

"HEY!" For some reason, Alan interrupted me in the middle of my rave about the skills of my family's servants.

"What is it?"

"Don't 'what is it' me! You're a lady, aren't you? And yet you... at this place, talk about un... under... underwe..." Alan, whose face was now beet-red, seemed to be saying something, but I couldn't catch the last part. He was red all the way up to his ears, and he was breathing heavily.

Is he tired from all the dancing? Maybe he has less stamina for this kind of thing, which is surprising. Or maybe he's just not used to it? When the dance ended, Alan still didn't seem like he'd recovered.

Next was the devilishly handsome Count Nicol. He was watched too, by both men and women. Although he was already going to the academy, being a year older than me, he'd still made time to show up at my party.

Nicol held out his hand elegantly, and soon I was dancing again. "You look wonderful, Lady Katarina," he said."

"Th-Thank... you. Very much."

A familiar, bewitching smile flitted onto his face, and as soon as it did, sighs of admiration came from the people around us. After knowing him for so many years, I had gotten used to his smile a little bit, but these other people weren't so lucky.

"Master Nicol is smiling... ever so faintly!" I could hear the whispers in the crowd. The powers of the Alluring Count were truly fearsome. I could imagine him walking around the academy, entrancing students left and right.

Nicol's lead was elegant and polite. Although he did have that seductive air, he really was a gentle and caring brother on the inside. He really stuck out from the other potential love interests of *Fortune Lover*. In fact, if I ever had the chance to go back to my previous life and play this game again, I would definitely explore his route first.

As I continued dancing with Nicol, I thought of something I wanted to ask him about. "Master Nicol, how do you feel about your life at the academy?"

"There have been no issues to date."

...*Ah*. As usual, our conversation didn't go very far. Although Nicol had opened up to me a little and seemed to become my true friend over the years, his silent demeanor had remained constant.

"...Um... have you made friends? Anyone you are close with, perhaps?" I said, deciding to bravely push on.

"...To a certain extent, yes," Nicol replied, after giving my question some thought. It seemed like he had to think a lot before answering, actually, but it was probably nothing to worry about.

"Well... Then have you found anyone you like, perhaps?"

Although Count Nicol was an impossibly alluring person, charming men and women alike, I hadn't heard any rumors about his love life. This was the perfect chance for me to ask more questions — for Sophia's sake, too, since she loved her brother so much. I'd asked about it casually, but...

"..."

Did Nicol just go silent, suddenly? Huh? Should I not have brought it up?

Hmm... what should I do? What should I say next? I started to panic.

"...Yes. I have," said Nicol abruptly.

"Wha?!" Surprised, I stared straight at Nicol. Sure enough, a very slight blush was now creeping up on his face.

So... that means he does have someone he likes? Even though I was the one who asked the question to begin with, I really wasn't expecting him to come out and tell me like that. As far as I knew, Nicol wasn't close with anyone outside of the usual group who came to my manor. *Did he find someone he likes after going to the academy? Hmm.*

"Would that be someone at the academy?" I asked.

"...No, not quite."

Huh? No? Then who could it possibly be? "Um... well then, may I ask who it is...?"

"...That, I... I cannot answer."

"...Hm...?"

"It is someone I should not have feelings for, in truth. However... I am always wishing for their happiness."

"..." *The fact that Nicol has someone he likes is already surprising enough — and now I'm told that it's someone he shouldn't have feelings for?!*

208

Is this... f-forbidden love?! Who is it? Some noble lord's wife... or perhaps even a man?!

I didn't expect my lighthearted question to get such a heavy response. I never would have guessed that Nicol would be after someone else's wife... or a man...

Well, maybe it's nothing like that at all. Either way, I could never bring myself to tell his sister about it.

"I am sure that something will work out for you, Master Nicol," I said, hoping to ease his worries over this forbidden love of his. Nicol just smiled in response, though he still looked a little troubled.

And with that, I finished my dance with Nicol, who seemed a little worse for wear after the whole thing. Almost immediately a smiling Mary approached me.

"My heartfelt congratulations, Lady Katarina. You look gorgeous, truly," Mary said, looking at my made-up appearance that had taken all the dedication of my household's servants to prepare. Mary, in contrast to my villainess-looking self that had taken half a day to cover up, was always breathtaking.

"Lady Katarina... Congratulations." Emerging from behind Mary was Sophia, who was pretty enough to give even Mary a run for her money.

All these compliments had almost convinced me that I was pretty, but now, seeing these two, I know what a pretty girl actually looks like. Good thing I realized that before it got into my head!

"If I were a man, I would be able to dance with you too, Lady Katarina..." Mary said with adorably puffed-out cheeks.

"I would have liked to dance with you too, Mary," I said with my best smile.

"REALLY?! Well then, perhaps we could dance later... in secret...?"

Such a bold suggestion from my gentle friend!

"Huh? Well, sure, but I don't really know how to lead a dance…"
If I were dancing with Mary, I imagined that I'd be the one doing the
man's part and leading. But I knew there was no way I was capable
of that. It was already hard enough for me to get the lady's part right!

"Not to worry, Lady Katarina! I have prepared myself should
such an event come to pass! I know the gentleman's dance steps too!"

*Ah, Mary really is a shining example of an ideal noble lady. It's
just like her to know how to lead the dance too. She's in a league of her
own.* While I didn't really get what Mary meant by her "preparations,"
I assumed that she just spent her days preparing for all kinds of
activities in general.

"Well then… perhaps we could, after the party's done, in secret?"
I said. Two girls dancing in front of all these guests would cause
some gossip, so it would be better if we saved it for later.

"Yes… I would be most glad to, Lady Katarina," Mary said,
beaming.

But then a voice rose up from next to her. "Ohh… I want to
dance too…" For some reason, Sophia was sulking intensely. Did she
want to dance with Mary too? Well, she could have her turn after we
were finished.

Once the party was ending and most people had left, Mary and
I had our dance. Not surprisingly, she was great at it. Sophia said
she wanted to dance with me too, so we did, but I embarrassingly
bungled most of the steps.

And so, the evening concluded and I peacefully turned fifteen
without any more mishaps.

When winter rolled around, the countdown to entering the
academy began. The curriculum lasted for two years, and since I'd

be staying in the dormitories at the school for most of that time, I had to prepare a lot of luggage to take with me.

Since I was the daughter of a duke, most of these preparations were done by the servants of the house. But of course, I didn't feel like it was fair to make them do all the work. And anyway, all they were packing was dresses and jewelry and things like that. They didn't include my romance novels or farming equipment! So I decided to start packing my own bags.

Five servants from my household, including my personal maid Anne, would follow me to the academy. Although I told my parents that I could handle myself fine and didn't need servants, I was told that it was unbecoming for the daughter of a duke to say so.

In the end, I was forced to take five servants with me — the lowest possible number that was allowed. But I was worried about one of them.

I was concerned about Anne, who had been by my side since I was eight. She had been taking care of me these past seven years, and was eight years older than me. That would make her twenty-three years old, which was seen as a young age in my previous life. But in this world, women were expected to marry early. If someone waited until they were, say, twenty-five, that would be considered late.

While Anne was my family maid, she was also actually the oldest daughter of a baron. Apparently the lower-ranked aristocrats of this world sent their daughters off to higher noble houses to learn the ways of the world while earning their keep. So many of these families had the habit of sending out their eldest daughters to serve as maids — a sort of internship, I suppose.

Many of the maids in my entourage came from that kind of background. Naturally, they were dignified ladies that had clearly been raised with care. For instance, they screamed when I climbed trees, and promptly fainted when I caught snakes. Because of that, most of them didn't last very long in our house. Mother always scolded me like crazy whenever one of them left our service.

Yet amidst all that, Anne always stayed by my side and offered little snippets of criticism and advice. She was a very important person to me.

The message from Anne's family actually arrived a few years ago — one discussing her marriage. This made me panic, of course. If Anne left her position, yet another new maid would faint upon witnessing me climbing trees and things like that. I couldn't picture how my life would be without her. And so in my panic, I did the first thing that came to my mind…

…Which was to approach Anne's father, who had arrived at the manor to bring his daughter back for the marriage. I dramatically lowered my head and pleaded desperately, "Please, I need Anne by my side, I absolutely do!"

Seeing this, Anne's father was stunned, his expression frozen. And yet, I did succeed in convincing Anne's family to allow her to stay with me. Sometimes pleading can pay off after all.

In other words, I successfully canceled Anne's wedding arrangements. When Mother found out about the whole thing, I got in big trouble… But Anne just laughed and seemed to forget about the whole thing.

So I accepted Anne's kindness for what it was, and she stayed with me this whole time. But now that she was twenty-three, I felt bad for making her stay this long. That was why I decided that she should return to her family's estate once it was time for me to go to the academy. Or at least, that's what I thought, until…

"If I were gone, young miss, who would take care of you? Of course I will be accompanying you to the academy," Anne said.

To be honest, I was really worried at the prospect of having to go to the academy and wait for Catastrophic Bad Ends to creep up on me without Anne by my side. So in the end, I accepted Anne's kindness again and agreed to have her come with me.

Thank you so much, Anne.

"Young miss… if I may ask, what exactly is this?" Anne asked as she pulled out some gardening overalls from my pile of luggage.

"Oh, that? My gardening overalls, of course."

"Gardening…? Correct me if I am wrong, but do you intend to grow crops and till fields in the academy as well?"

"Of course I do! After all, if I stop gardening for two years, I'll never become a good farmer!" I replied, full of confidence and vigor.

Anne, however, looked as if all the strength had been sapped out of her. "…But… why would the daughter of a duke ever become a farmer, of all things…?"

"Just in case certain things come to pass!"

"And what exactly are these 'things'?! Please, young miss. Do not tell me that you intend on bringing your hoe as well."

"Yes, that too! After all, there is no guarantee that I'll be able to find one at the academy."

"…Please, young miss…"

Anne and I went back and forth like this for quite a while, with me trying to put the necessary items in my suitcase, and Anne actively preventing me from doing so.

Winter passed, and spring slowly approached…

My name is Anne Shelley. I was born in the rural outskirts, to the family of a baron. At fifteen years of age, I was sent to Claes Manor to learn the ways of the world.

It was there that I became the personal maid of Katarina Claes, the only child and daughter of the Claes family. When I first met with Lady Katarina, I recalled her having quite the cute face. Her upwards-slanting almond-like eyes gave her a determined look.

As expected of the daughter of a noble family, Lady Katarina was very spoiled, and had a selfish, arrogant personality. A few months into my service, however, Lady Katarina tripped and fell during a walk at the royal castle grounds, and most unfortunately hit her head on a rock.

As a result of the incident, Lady Katarina hurt her head. The impact even left a scar. Perhaps that was the reason why she slept for quite a few days, all the while with a high fever.

However, when she awoke, it was as if she were a different person altogether. The self-absorbed Lady Katarina was gone, instead replaced by a calm, caring little lady. She even showed unprecedented awareness and care towards her servants, as if she were reborn as a more compassionate person.

The young miss' personality had changed completely due to the impact to her head and the fever that followed. While the servants were equally surprised and grateful by the sudden change that had come over her, Lady Katarina only remained like this during her short period of bed rest.

After the fever receded, Lady Katarina sat up — and then proceeded to become even more problematic than she was before this entire affair.

Having awoken from her rest, Lady Katarina ran all the way to the library, asking many questions of the servants, and sometimes making outlandish requests of them. Just as we thought it had all passed, the young miss had yet another demand — that she take up lessons in both magic and the sword.

While her effort in the field was commendable, the footwork aspect of her swordplay lessons did not quite go as well — it almost seemed like the young miss would slice her own leg off before cutting the opponent, and we all collectively held our breaths.

Next, she declared that she would practice her magic, and then promptly dressed up in a set of gardening overalls, took up a hoe, and started tilling the earth. Lady Katarina Claes was readying a field in the Claes Manor gardens.

After spending quite some time in the gardens, she would then hike up her dress and start climbing trees. The young miss also took up fishing, of all things, in the small river that ran through the grounds. She would eventually almost push the local fish population close to extinction.

Problem after problem arose, just like that. While Madam Claes became progressively angrier with each transgression, the young miss was firmly set in her ways. While she would have a downcast look about her immediately after she was given a scolding, she would be all recovered the very next day. It would seem that Lady Katarina had the mysterious ability to forget about all the reprimands and criticisms directed at her after a good night's sleep.

At fifteen years of age, the young miss had unfortunately remained very much the same. She did, however, stop climbing trees eventually.

There was one incident where Lady Katarina picked up a mushroom growing in the garden, claiming that it was "absolutely edible." That was, however, unfortunately not the case, and the young miss suffered a bout of food poisoning, in addition to a good scolding from the madam.

After this, the young miss suddenly announced that she would study farming methodologies, immersing herself in books on agriculture. Before long, she had started on a mission to expand the fields in the gardens.

It was as if she hadn't changed at all — not in the slightest, ever since she was eight years old. Although I had been in her service for seven years, and was always by her side, I still could not predict what Lady Katarina would think of next.

However, even though the young miss was quite the troublemaker, she did enjoy immense popularity amongst... certain parties. For instance, Jeord Stuart, the third prince and Lady Katarina's fiancé. The accomplished and beautiful prince took a great liking to her and very much enjoyed spending time with her, judging by the adoring expression on his face.

Lady Katarina, however, did not seem to understand the Prince's feelings, not even with such an expression directed at her. Dense as the young miss was, I could not help but be overcome with fear when she unexpectedly approached the prince — to cancel their engagement, of all things!

The scar on Lady Katarina's head was the reason why this engagement existed in the first place, and now that scar had perfectly healed. I remembered the day of her injury, back when she was eight years old, so I was happy for her when she realized that the scar was gone.

However, never in my wildest dreams would I have thought that the young miss would use this as a reason to cancel the engagement — or say what she did to the prince. That was when I first realized that Lady Katarina did not have a clue about Prince Jeord's affection towards her, in spite of all his actions.

"Prince Jeord, the scar on my forehead has completely vanished. As such, you no longer need to take responsibility for me. I wouldn't mind if the engagement were canceled," Lady Katarina said, happily smiling!

The prince's eyes opened wide in surprise. Then he smiled reassuringly, but I noticed that his eyes were not smiling at all. "Is that so? Well then, if you would please show me."

Slowly approaching the young miss, Prince Jeord parted her hair forcefully, exposing her forehead. It was as she said — the scar had completely vanished.

"No, Katarina. There is still quite the scar, from what I can see," Prince Jeord said, all the while staring at Lady Katarina's perfectly smooth and unscarred skin.

"Wha? But I've checked many times in the mirror... Anne helped, too..."

Oh, young miss. You mustn't. Please don't turn this way...

"I would suppose you were both mistaken. A scar yet remains here. Do you not think so too?" Prince Jeord said, turning to me with his charming smile that his eyes did not share. All I could do was nod my head rapidly, agreeing wholeheartedly with him.

In the end, the now non-existent scar was brought back onto the table by Prince Jeord, who promptly ended the discussion with a single statement. "So you see, there will be no cancellations with regards to our engagement." All the while looking at us with those unsmiling eyes of this.

It was a terrifying moment for me — I felt like several years of my life had been shaved off of my poor heart.

And then there was the matter of Lady Katarina's adopted brother, Keith Claes. Although he was a skinny and gloomy child

217

when we first met him, the young master had become a beautiful youth as the years went by, and was now the apple of many a lady's eye.

He was exceedingly popular with women, perhaps on account of how he was always gentle and kind to every woman he met. And now, having reached this age, the young master could not help but be charming. To tell the truth, many of the servants had fallen head over heels for him.

Master Keith, however, only had eyes for the young miss. He would follow Lady Katarina about almost daily, offering her support and cleaning up her occasional social faux pas. The gaze of burning passion in his eyes, directed at the young miss, was evidently not one of platonic sibling love.

However Lady Katarina, being dense as she was, hardly noticed this. Perhaps she simply did not have the faculties to understand the young master's charms, which seemed likely, knowing the young miss.

"...They say I'm charming... but it is meaningless, isn't it? If the one you love hardly notices it at all..."

That was what I heard as I happened upon the young master one day, mumbling to himself with a gloomy expression on his face. It was a saddening sight.

Eventually, the young master would side with Madam Claes, forming the "Katarina could not possibly perform the duties of a queen!" camp. Try as they might to cancel the engagement between Katarina and Prince Jeord, however, their efforts have not yet borne fruit. As far as I know, their efforts continue in the shadows to this day...

And then there was the fourth prince of the kingdom, Alan Stuart — the twin brother of Prince Jeord. He, too, only had Lady Katarina in his eyes.

He was said to be a genius of music, and his many performances drew steadily multiplying crowds. The Prince would invite Lady Katarina each time, without fail. There was an unmistakable gleam in his eyes — favor for the young miss, surely, when he looked upon her.

The one fault with Prince Alan, however, was the fact that he was almost as dense as the young lady herself. For seven long years he stared in her general direction — and yet had no awareness of it at all.

The sight of the Prince who obviously had feelings for Lady Katarina, yet clearly did not understand his own feelings, was quite sad to behold. While I was originally exasperated, I began to feel pity for his situation.

However, I did understand that this wasn't just a matter of Prince Alan being particularly dense. Those who already had an eye for the young miss, such as Prince Jeord and Master Keith, set about ensuring that Alan would never notice how he himself felt.

Of these individuals, the most skilled amongst them had to be Prince Alan's fiancée herself, Lady Mary Hunt. I would understand if she wanted to hinder the two's relationship to keep Prince Alan for herself... The truth, however, was the opposite of that — after all, Lady Mary Hunt herself was a woman after the young miss' heart.

Lady Mary Hunt, had changed drastically since her first meeting with the young miss. While she was originally nervous and shy, her name had spread far in noble society these seven years, and she was heralded as the very image of a noble lady — a far cry from the girl she used to be.

That very same lady, however, really did have quite the thing for the young miss. If I had to describe it… For example, Lady Mary had no qualms about the idea of canceling the young miss' engagement with the Prince, and then dragging her to some faraway place so she could have her all to herself. That was how deep it went.

Lady Mary's plan had begun quite a few years ago. At that time, she announced to the young miss that she was not capable of being queen, saying "I am not at all suited to such an important role as queen." This filled the young miss with unease. After all, even the most perfect noble lady now had reservations about the idea of marrying a prince.

Upon hearing that, the young miss echoed Lady Mary's sentiments, announcing that, "Ah, then it would be impossible for me, too. What am I going to do?"

Lady Mary's response to the young miss' unease was swift. Holding her hands, she smiled gently, saying, "Well then, perhaps we could both break our engagements… and the two of us could escape to some faraway land."

At first, I had assumed that this was all some sort of joke… until Lady Mary started detailing the tools used in this grand escape. It was then that I understood just how serious she was. To phrase it simply, Lady Mary Hunt was absolutely serious and willing to cancel both engagements, sweep the young miss off her feet, and carry her to some faraway land.

Lady Katarina, being as dense as she was, hardly noticed Mary's feelings. Even now, she speaks of Lady Mary as a friend, with a warm smile. "Mary is such a gentle girl…"

And with this, her adopted brother, the twin princes, and even the noble lady engaged to one of the princes were now after her affections. The young miss, of course, knew absolutely nothing about all this.

She then gained yet more admirers — one of which being the royal chancellor's son, Master Nicol Ascart. He too was hopelessly lost in the young miss' eyes.

He was quite the impressive boy, with his jet-black eyes and hair, doll-like features, and alluring aura. He had his official debut to noble society late last year, and even had a fanclub following. His so-called fanclub, however, was not only filled with women — but also a fair number of men.

While Prince Jeord, Prince Alan, and Master Keith were all beautiful and handsome in their own ways, there was something different about Master Nicol — to be specific, that bewitching aura of his. This was why the young miss referred to him as the "Alluring Count" day in and day out.

Master Nicol was, however, usually a very stoic individual. He hardly talked about himself, much less spoke very much at all. Even amongst his large following, few had seen him ever show any hint of emotion.

That very same Master Nicol, however, often smiled at Lady Katarina — a truly happy, blissful smile. It was truly a force of nature, that smile of his. Those who bear witness to it inadvertently become weak at the knees. In fact, many of my fellow maids had become effectively useless after witnessing such a spectacle.

As expected of the young miss, however, she remained perfectly oblivious to this, even though she was the only one who caused Master Nicol to behave in this way...

"I have to protect Mary and Keith from being bewitched by the Alluring Count...!" she would mutter to herself.

It would seem that the young miss, being impervious to Master Keith's charms, had proven to be equally invulnerable to the destructive power of Master Nicol's faint smile…

Lastly, there was the sister of Master Nicol — Sophia Ascart. Needless to say, she was very fond of the young miss as well. Much like Lady Katarina, Lady Sophia had a great love for romance novels, and often came to Claes Manor to bring the young miss book recommendations.

Lady Sophia, having long noticed her brother's feelings for the young miss, often extolled Nicol's virtues in her presence. As expected of Lady Katarina, however, she hardly understood Sophia's motivations for doing this, and quickly attributed it to her love for her brother.

And just like that, many people began to gather around the problem child that was Lady Katarina. Much like Master Keith, the young miss was very much a subconscious charmer.

And she had more than just friends of the noble variety. Even the difficult and usually reserved head gardener, Tom, seemed to enjoy himself in Lady Katarina's presence. The somewhat distant head maid, who was strict with herself and her colleagues, was also different in front of the young miss — she often wore a peaceful expression, one that I had not seen before.

Regardless of her age, the problems she causes, and her eccentricities, Lady Katarina attracts people to her side without fail. What exactly is it that pulls so many people to her…?

To tell the truth… I can answer that question easily myself.

I, Anne Shelley, was born due to an affair between Baron Shelley and a servant of the Shelley family — my mother. I was kept separate from the Baron's main household, and was instead raised in a small home on the grounds.

CHAPTER 6: FINALLY, MY BIRTHDAY IS HERE!

The Baron was a fickle man, my mother said. He had only slept with her a few times before I was born into this world. *"Do as the Baron says... act in such a way that will make him like you. Never, ever think about going against him..."* This was something that she always repeated to me as I grew up.

I followed those instructions. I did what the Baron said and what my mother wished for me to do, never going against either of them. I lived my life for the sole purpose of earning the Baron's favor.

Perhaps because of my quiet obedience, I was never called to the main residence, nor was the Baron ever cruel to me. All things considered, I was able to live a somewhat peaceful life.

However, that would all end one day in the year of my fifteenth birthday. Without warning, the room next to mine caught fire, and the fire soon spread to the surroundings. Although I somehow managed to escape, I suffered large burns to my back, and my mother lost her life in the disaster.

I was in shock from the sudden turn my life had taken. It was then that it happened — for the first time since I was born, I was summoned to the main residence by the Baron.

"I have heard that your back has been terribly scarred. Now that you are damaged, I can no longer use you as an instrument for political marriages. I have no more need for you. Get out of this house," the Baron said to me, as if he were speaking casually of the changes in the weather. I could not even find any words to protest.

Up until now, I had tried all my life to earn the Baron's favor. I had been so proud of myself, thinking that an absence of cruelty meant that he had accepted me. But I was wrong. The Baron was not cruel to me simply because he was not interested in me. To him, I was nothing more than a tool. And now that I had become like this, I was... no longer needed.

And just like that, I lost my abode and my reason for existing, almost overnight. The Claes family, a distant relation of mine, just so happened to be looking for maids — and that was how I ended up there, learning the ways of the world.

I eventually was assigned the position of personal maid to Lady Katarina Claes, the sole daughter of the Claes family. Lady Katarina was spoiled, selfish, and arrogant towards her servants. Most maids assigned to her did not last very long, but that was not the case for me.

After all, I was different from the other girls, who could simply return to their homes and search for another place to learn their lessons. I no longer had a place to go back to. If I were chased out of Claes Manor, I would be out on the streets.

I lived as I had always lived — I sought to earn her favor, just like I did with the Baron and my mother, never going against anything she said. Whatever Lady Katarina wanted to have, I gave her. Whatever she wanted to hear, I told her. I never went against her in any way. I became what my masters wanted me to become, shaped by their desires.

As long as I did as I was told, Lady Katarina's mood slowly improved, and the days began to pass without any problems. After all, this was how I had always lived. The only thing that changed was the person I served. All I had to do was become a new tool in Claes Manor.

However, following the impact to her head and her feverish slumber, the awakened Lady Katarina changed. She was no longer arrogant, and no longer selfish. She no longer sought praise from me, or words of approval. She climbed the trees and tilled the fields — a decidedly unusual noble lady.

I no longer knew how to earn her favor, or how I should react to her actions. Having lived my entire life telling people what they wanted to hear, and being what they wanted me to be, I found myself at a loss. I had no real will of my own.

And so, as I remained lost in thought about how to interact with this suddenly changed Lady Katarina... I realized that I soon began to speak on my own accord. Although I no longer was full of praise for her, nor did I affirm everything she said and did, Lady Katarina was never cruel to me. I found myself slowly starting to respect her.

For the first time in my life, I received a birthday present. A sheaf of paper tickets with the words "shoulder massage ticket" written on them in messy letters. And wooden carvings of a strange, unidentified lifeform. All these were gifts from Lady Katarina, handed to me every year, and I kept all of them packed away safely.

The days I spent serving the unpredictable Lady Katarina were exhausting to say the least. However, compared to those fifteen-odd years that I spent living in that small house, this was something I could never have dreamed of — impossibly bright, vibrant, and happy days.

I want to stay by Lady Katarina's side for as long as I can. I no longer remember when I started thinking this way.

After spending a few years in the Claes family, a letter arrived from an individual who had not contacted me all this time — Baron Shelley. The letter was curt: *"Your engagement has been arranged. Return to the estate at once."*

All the color drained from my face. *Engagement...? Even though I was told that I am no longer useful as an instrument for political marriage because of the burn scars on my back?*

Before, I would have rushed back to the estate immediately after receiving such a letter. I was just a tool. A tool that could not dream of going against its master, the Baron. However... I was no longer the girl I was before. I wanted to stay here.

This was why I had ignored the letter… until Baron Shelley himself showed up at Claes Manor. I was summoned to the room where he was waiting, looking exactly as he had all those years ago.

"I found an eccentric, you see. Someone who has interest in you, regardless of the damage. Since you did not seem to understand my summons, I have personally shown up, to bring you back, of course," the Baron said, his twisted expression seemingly suggesting that I thank him for his efforts.

The man that I was engaged to had many bad rumors swirling around him in noble society — a viscount with more lovers than one could count on both hands. Baron Shelley was certainly being paid a handsome sum to arrange such a marriage. But I knew I would never be happy in such an arrangement.

Was I mistaken in thinking that a tool could ever be happy in the first place? A sudden chill came over my body, as if all the blood had been sucked out of it that very moment.

"Why do you dally? I have already spoken to Duke Claes. Make the arrangements now! We are returning to the estate," the Baron said, seemingly displeased at my silence.

Ah… with this, it will all end. My happy days will be over, and I will become nothing more than a tool once more.

I want to stay here. I want to spend more time here, by Lady Katarina's side…

And that was when it happened.

"Excuse me!" With a prompt greeting and a knock, the Lady Katarina herself burst into the room in a huff. "You are Anne's father, yes?" she said, directing her sharp gaze towards the Baron.

"…Y-Yes." The Baron himself was at a loss, apparently surprised by the sudden entrance of this young girl.

"Please! Please rethink this whole affair about Anne's marriage engagement!" Lady Katarina said, suddenly gripping me by the arm. "Please, I need Anne by my side, I absolutely do! I want her to stay! If you take her away… I won't stand for it! I can't!" she shouted, ignoring the Baron's surprised expression as she said what she came here to say.

The sight before me was surreal — it was like I was a spectator, gazing into a foreign world. I could feel the heat of Lady Katarina's grip. Slowly, the warmth from her hand warmed up my body.

I had lived all my life simply pleasing my betters. It was here at Claes Manor, however… here by Lady Katarina's side, that I first found my own will, my own voice.

Somewhere along the line, I had stopped being just a mere tool. No longer a tool, but just… just Anne Shelley. And even so, Lady Katarina said she needed me. That she wanted me by her side.

Before I knew it, the young miss' warmth filled my entire being. I found that it warmed up my head especially. I desperately held back the tears that were threatening to spill forth from my eyes at any moment.

Due to Lady Katarina's actions that day, the engagement itself was now called into question. A short while after this incident, Duke Claes somehow found out about the negative circumstances surrounding my engagement, and in turn called off the entire deal with the Baron's family.

No words could describe the gratitude I felt for Duke Claes. In fact, the Duke himself even suggested an alternative. "If you would like, I could put the word out for a proper suitor — someone who would treat you well," he said.

Even so, I chose to stay by Lady Katarina's side. I remained Lady Katarina's personal maid at Claes Manor up until now.

Regardless of her age, the problems she causes, and her eccentricities, Lady Katarina attracts people to her side without fail. What exactly is it that pulls so many people to her...?

To tell the truth... I can answer that question easily. After all, I know better than anyone else could possibly know...

I was just a tool to be used, but Lady Katarina treated me, Anne Shelley, as a human being. I would never forget the warmth of her grip, or the words she spoke on my behalf that day.

I will definitely accompany her to the Academy of Magic in the coming spring. Although the young miss claims that she would be "just fine"... she can hardly put on her own dress correctly. If left to her own devices, her hair would be messy and undone — there is no way she would be "just fine," nor was this fitting for the daughter of a duke.

"Of course I will be accompanying you to the academy," I said, despite Lady Katarina's stunned expression.

"But then, don't you want to get married, Anne? I don't think I could ask you to stay..."

It would seem that the young miss was even concerned about my marital status! Talking about weddings and such. I couldn't help but laugh a little. After all, I had no desires or expectations for marriage. I only had one wish.

"If I were gone, young miss, who would take care of you? Of course I will be accompanying you to the academy."

At my words, Lady Katarina herself started laughing.

Even if Lady Katarina did become queen in the future, and had to live at the royal castle with Prince Jeord... Even if Lady Mary took her away to some faraway land. Regardless of what the future held, I would always be by the young miss' side.

After all, this was where I belonged... This was where I was happy: standing next to Lady Katarina.

I only have one wish, my lady. And that is to live on, always by your side.

After my birthday party ended, a sense of peace finally returned to my surroundings. With all my party dress preparations and dance lessons done, I could finally catch my breath.

In fact, I was planning to tend to the fields that I'd been neglecting for a while. So for the first time in what felt like forever, I put on my overalls and bandana and walked out to the fields decked out in my farming gear.

To prepare for this year's summer harvest, I wanted to scatter the fertilizer that Jeord had given me for my birthday. Keith was here too, since I had asked for his help. As we were about to get started, Jeord showed up.

"Hello, Katarina. I see you are hard at work today as well."

"Oh, Prince Jeord! Thank you for coming to my birthday party last night, and for your birthday gift. I wanted to set about using the fertilizer you gave me immediately."

"I see. I am glad that you were able to put it to good use so quickly. Well worth the effort to gift you what you requested, if I may say so... In truth, I had wanted to give you a dress, or perhaps an accessory you could wear on your person... but knowing you, Katarina, you would hardly accept such a gift," Jeord said with a somewhat bitter smile on his face.

That was true. Originally, Jeord always wanted to send me a dress or some sort of accessory, but I always refused on the spot. My father, who loved me to bits, constantly showered me with dresses and accessories already — there was a small pile of them in my closet. Honestly, I felt like there were a few too many garments in my room...

If I were like Katarina from the original setting of *Fortune Lover*, I would have loved changing in and out of pretty dresses, sporting a new one each day. In fact, she wouldn't have minded having a surplus of dresses to choose from.

Unfortunately, I was a different person from my game counterpart. I didn't like fancy dresses at all because they were so annoying to move around in. In fact, living life in tight-fitting, frilly, restrictive dresses day in and day out sounded like a nightmare to me. I couldn't see it as anything but some kind of twisted punishment.

And anyway, I was mostly focused on my work in the fields, and I had good gardening overalls for that. I didn't need the small mountain of dresses tucked away somewhere in my closet. I felt the same way about accessories, too. If I were to lose some expensive piece of jewelry or something while working in the fields, it would be quite a total fiasco.

Because of this, I decided to inform my close friends to not send me presents like that. Jeord, of course, was one of them. He heeded my request, and presented me with the fertilizer I asked for instead.

"However, Katarina, you are already fifteen years of age this year. It is about time that your status is made clear to those around you. After all, you belong to me — perhaps I should send you some garments befitting your station," Jeord said thoughtfully.

Garments befitting my station? Me belonging to Jeord? Hmm... What does he mean?

"I think everyone already knows that I'm your fiancée..." In fact, word of it had spread so far that you'd be hard-pressed to find someone who didn't know. Of course, that was the whole point of the engagement, after all; to deflect suitors.

"Perhaps it is so, Katarina. However, many are not quite convinced of the reality of it — regardless of their knowledge on the matter."

I supposed Jeord had a point. I wasn't breathtakingly beautiful like Mary, and I had this villainess face of mine to deal with. I wasn't that impressive compared to the high-spec people around me — hence the gossip. Specifically, gossip that said Jeord and I weren't a good match even if my social class was suitable.

But I wasn't interested in challenging their opinions or convincing them. In fact, if any of them wanted to take over my position of fiancée, I'd hand over the title happily. Still, I couldn't just tell Jeord something like, *"Being your fiancée sucks. I pass."* Instead, all I did was smile vaguely. That was what I was doing now, hoping to resolve the problem.

"What exactly is it that you are doing…?" Keith said, coming between me and Jeord with an intense expression.

Hmm? Does he feel left out because I didn't include him in the discussion?

"Hello, Keith Claes. To come between two who are engaged and interrupt their rendezvous… quite the tactless maneuver, no? And what is with that intense expression of yours? Hardly fitting for your pretty face, Keith."

"Unfortunately, Prince Jeord, it seems that the only one who thinks of this meeting as a rendezvous is you. To answer your question, I have adopted this intense expression in place of my Big Sister. After all, she has absolutely no sense of danger… especially when it comes to particularly nasty bugs."

"A nasty bug, you say? I wonder who that could be?"

"...A most unscrupulous individual who engaged in questionable acts in the middle of a dance floor, Prince Jeord."

"Hmm. Is that right? I have no idea who that could possibly be."

"You dare say that with those very lips?!"

"But of course. After all, she is my fiancée. Exactly how questionable is it to leave your own mark on something that belongs to you?"

"And who is it that you say belongs to you?! Big Sister is still a fiancée at this point in time, nothing more!"

It seemed like Keith and Jeord had started a heated discussion on a subject that I didn't understand. *Is this how it feels to be left out...? Hm, it does feel pretty lonely.*

I guess I should start working the fields on my own, then, I thought as I embraced my newfound agricultural exile.

"Lady Katarina!" Turning around upon hearing a familiar, bright voice, I caught sight of Mary and her vibrant smile. Following close behind her were Sophia and Alan.

"Hmm? Did you all decide to come visit together?" Although they were a common sight on the grounds, it was rare for my friends to visit all in one group.

"I invited them, you see."

"You did, Mary?"

"Yes. I had heard from Master Keith that some questionable events came to pass at the party. I felt that it would be prudent to strengthen our defenses — and there is strength in numbers, so I invited Lady Sophia. Prince Alan came too."

What exactly happened at the party? I had no idea what they were talking about. *Keith told Mary about it instead of his own sister? That's so cold! I suddenly feel so lonely...*

Also, Mary just bringing Alan along for whatever Keith told her seems a little absurd... well, it seems like Alan himself doesn't mind, so I guess that's okay. But honestly... everything going on lately really goes against what I knew about Fortune Lover.

"On another note, Lady Katarina. Did you enjoy the books that you have been gifted for your birthday?"

"Ah, that's right. Lady Mary, Lady Sophia, Prince Alan. Allow me to express my heartfelt thanks for your wonderful gifts. I've already finished one of them!"

Alan, Mary, and Sophia had come together to choose a selection of amazing books for my birthday. The girls did most of the work, of course. Alan never knew what to send me each year, so he'd always follow Mary's instructions.

This year, Mary had decided on a book as a gift, and had then apparently approached Sophia, who usually gave me books as gifts. The two apparently came together and had a discussion before choosing this year's birthday presents. I was overjoyed to get so many pieces of "high literature" for my birthday.

"I am glad that you are happy with your gifts, Lady Katarina. As I expected, something that remains in one's hands is much more fitting as a gift. At least, when compared to something that simply disappears into the soil."

"And would that be a jibe directed at me, Lady Mary Hunt?" Jeord, who had been locked in a heated argument with Keith mere moments ago, apparently decided to join this discussion too.

"Oh, if it isn't Prince Jeord. I did not quite see you there. I hope you are well?" Mary said, curtsying in an impossibly elegant way. Classic Mary, the lady amongst noble ladies. I wished I were more like her.

Seeing her elegant greeting, even Jeord couldn't help but break into a smile. "Ha ha. Surely you jest, Lady Mary. I heard you loud and clear. It would seem like you are here with the express purpose of disturbing my and Katarina's private time."

"Oh, was I a disturbance? Do pardon me. All I wanted to do was spend some pleasant time with Lady Katarina."

"Lady Mary. Are you not my brother's fiancée? Perhaps you should be sharing some pleasant time with Alan instead?"

"But of course! That is why I have invited Prince Alan as well. Appearances, yes?"

"Ah, Lady Mary. To think that you were so lovable in your younger years. It would seem that your personality becomes more and more... interesting, with each passing year."

"Oh? It is an honor that you think so highly of me. However, I would still not be able to rival someone like you, Prince Jeord."

"But alas. You are merely being humble, my good lady."

It seemed that Jeord and Mary had now gotten into their own intense discussion. In fact, Keith had started cheering for Mary at some point, "Do your best, Lady Mary!" Meanwhile, Alan seemed puzzled upon hearing his name. "Hmm...? Appearances...?"

Excluding me again! Didn't all of you come to my manor to spend time with me?

To make things worse, they're all talking about difficult things I could never understand! I've never felt so lonely... I was starting to sulk.

"On another note, Lady Katarina... What did you think of my brother's gift to you...?" Sophia asked, smiling.

My lonely brooding was blown away in an instant by her radiant smile. "Ah yes, I really quite enjoyed it. Please tell Master Nicol that

I really liked the cute necklace he sent me," I replied, smiling back at Sophia.

"NECKLACE?!" For some reason, the four that were leaving me out of their conversations all said the same thing and turned to stare at me.

"Katarina. What exactly is this… 'necklace'?"

"But you are not fond at all of accessories, Big Sister. Did you not reject all such gifts?"

"Yes, yes. You said that you have no use for them and that you would therefore not accept them! Was that not the case?"

"Uh yeah, I heard the same thing from Mary…"

Everyone in the garden seemed shocked. I mean, that was true. I wasn't interested in accessories and dresses, so I turned them all down. However…

"…Actually, it was a necklace that was featured in one of the stories I read. And it didn't have any gems or anything like that, so I happily accepted it."

Yes, Nicol's birthday gift was the necklace that one of my favorite romance novel protagonists wore. Even though I didn't usually like accessories of any kind, my otaku tendencies made me weak to things that showed up in books or stories that I liked. *"It's just like that one character!"* I'd say excitedly.

"I actually like it so much that I have it on today, under my gardening overalls!" I lowered my collar ever so slightly, showing the necklace to my gathered friends. For some reason, all of them immediately made similarly intense faces.

Ah, I was worried about this. It must be a social faux pas to wear something like this under farming clothes!

"Eheheh. I was the one who gave my brother the advice, Lady Katarina. After all, he's the only one who's a year older, and he is always away. It's not very fair, you see..." Sophia said with an innocent smile.

Seeing her smile, my other four friends stood silently, as rooted to the spot as my crops.

Hello, this is Yamaguchi Satoru. Thank you very much for purchasing this book.

This work was originally submitted to the novel submission site "Shousetsuka ni Narou" in July of 2014, and was then serialized. I have all my readers to thank for my work being compiled into a book — and as such would like to extend my sincere thanks to the fans who have read my works on the site. Thank you very much.

Well then... the title of this book is quite long, isn't it? *My Next Life as a Villainess: All Routes Lead to Doom! Volume 1*. Even the supervisor of the editing department said, "It's the longest among all the works we have."

And as for the book's contents... it's exactly like the title says! The protagonist has been reincarnated as an antagonist character in an otome game called *Fortune Lover* that she was playing before her untimely death. She must overcome all the Catastrophic Bad Ends, and work hard to stay alive and well.

The protagonist, Katarina, isn't exceptionally beautiful, smart, or magically inclined. She's quite the disappointing main character, isn't she? But she has a creative mind, and tries her best to do what she can. I would be very glad if you, my dear readers, could continue watching over her warmly.

With regards to the illustrations for this book, I would like to thank Hidaka Nami-sama for their cute illustrations of Katarina and the other rival characters, as well as the cool Jeord and the many other romance interests.

When I first set eyes on these character designs, I was overwhelmed by just how splendid they were. Hidaka Nami-sama, thank you very much for your wonderful illustrations.

Lastly, I would also like to thank the supervisor of the editing department, who gave me a lot of advice, as I was quite clueless. I would also like to thank everyone who has helped with the publishing of this book — I thank them from the bottom of my heart.

Again, thank you very much, everyone.

Yamaguchi Satoru